My ChEMiCAL RoMaNCe
Something Incredible
This Way Comes

My Chemical Romance

Something Incredible This Way Comes

Paul Stenning

Independent Music Press

Published in 2006 by
INDEPENDENT MUSIC PRESS
Independent Music Press is an imprint of I.M. P. Publishing Limited
This Work is Copyright © I. M. P. Publishing Ltd 2006

My Chemical Romance: Something Incredible This Way Comes
by Paul Stenning

British Library Cataloguing-in-Publication Data.
A catalogue for this book is available from The British Library.

ISBN 0-9549704-5-4

Cover Design by Fresh Lemon.
Edited by Martin Roach.

Printed in the UK.

Independent Music Press
P.O. Box 69, Church Stretton, Shropshire SY6 6WZ

Visit us on the web at: www.impbooks.com
or at: www.myspace.com/independentmusicpress
For a free catalogue, e-mail us at: info@impbooks.com
Fax: 01694 720049

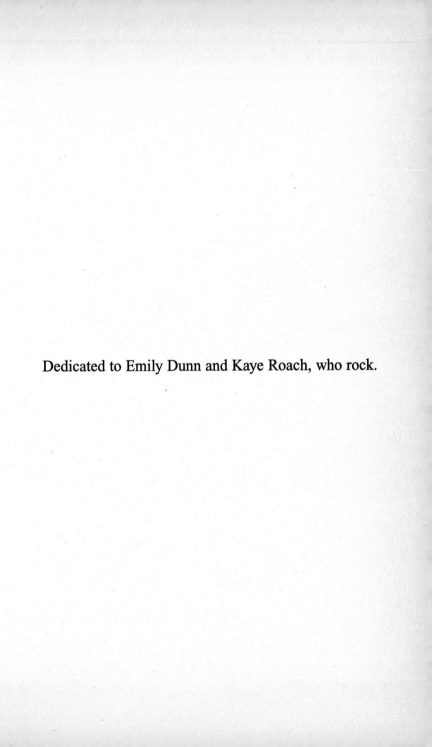

Dedicated to Emily Dunn and Kaye Roach, who rock.

Introduction

In a period of just four years, New Jersey's My Chemical Romance have progressed from being merely another new band on the rock scene to eclipsing all comers with their own brand of tortured dark rock. Given their original image – that of copious dark eyeliner and coiffured hair – it should come as no surprise that they have been lumped into every category from emo to goth. Considering their vigorously heavy sound, one could also make a claim for MCR as a heavy metal band.

In fact, MCR seek inspiration from just about any form of music, so it's no wonder their sound is difficult to pin down. Between them the five musical assassins draw motivation from The Misfits, David Bowie, The Smiths, Iron Maiden, The Cure, Green Day and Black

Flag. "There's such a wide variety of taste in the band," vocalist Gerard Way told *Crush Music* magazine. "We like melodies. We're a band with a lot of duality. We have a light side and a dark side and we just try to join the two. If a song is extra catchy or poppy, I will [make] sure the lyrics are so fucked up and dark that you can't play that song on the radio."

In short, with My Chemical Romance diversity comes naturally – as does the angst that oozes from the speakers with every note wrung from the vengeful axes of Ray Toro and Frank Iero, every lyric uttered by Gerard and each click of the rhythm section of drummer Bob Bryar and (Gerard's brother) bassist Mikey Way. MCR have been compared to such acts as Thursday and Cursive, yet this is to do them a disservice. The MCR experience is a very different beast – taut, writhing and leering at insignificant others as it leaves them behind. Gerard's impassioned vocals make the group's sound instantly identifiable as the New Jersey quintet, while the comic-strip-style drawings that characterise MCR's equally distinctive artwork are also credited to the band's front man.

The group also shine in their passionate lyrics, and their willingness to address the darkest sides of life. The innate humanity of Gerard's words, governed by his heart rather than his head, gives MCR a unique advantage over virtually all their peers. The broken hearts he sings about are not simply for show; they are as much a part of the band experience as a guitar and an amplifier. Those lyrics ooze conviction and courage –

and it is only natural for the group to complement them, musically, with heartfelt bombast. As a result, the most familiar line My Chemical Romance hear from their fans is, "Your music saved my life."

My Chemical Romance has several other advantages over most alternative rock bands out there. They are intelligent, free-thinking individuals. They value their fans and are happy to provide them with not only autographs but also minutes – sometimes hours – of their precious time and respect each and every one of their devotees as if they were family. This respect extends to journalists and reporters too – a habit many other bands would do well to imitate. The Way Brothers and Co. are always happy to answer questions, to give insight and to explain, often with brutal honesty, the nature of their lyrics and their performance. Despite an abundance of repeated, innately dull questions, the group always answer with a refreshing attitude, as if it were their first ever interview.

Given the band's swift rise to fame, this is perhaps understandable. MCR are still in their infancy with regard to self-promotion and the baring of their soul and their secrets. Fans can only hope this inspirational and fresh outlook, which is very refreshing, can continue for the duration of the band's career. It would be a shame to see the enthusiastic five-piece gradually becoming tainted by the rock-star life and turning into cynics – a corporate rock act. Yet given the experiences My Chemical Romance have already overcome, and throughout which they have remained focused, the attitudes of the music world they inhabit would be unlikely to convert this bunch of level-headed, smart-talking individuals into a lump of ignorant musos.

The band has collectively survived broken bones, broken hearts, heavy drinking, drug use, chipped teeth, lacerations, infections, liver damage and a host of other physical ailments. This is a group that gives everything for the cause and for the legions of fans, which are increasing with every note of the radio-played hit singles My Chemical Romance has so far enjoyed. Such bands can often self-destruct – too much excess to remain focused enough for the long haul. Yet that fault is not in the make-up of the MCR members – these tendencies expressed themselves early enough for the individuals concerned to work them out of their systems and move on; now the only damage done to the bodies of those involved is on stage, with the whip of a guitar or the fist of a numbskull security guard. My Chemical Romance has already experienced the kind of things that ultimately cause most bands to self-destruct, and with the core of the quintet being the two brothers, there is no likelihood of a parting of the Ways. Indeed, despite their brief recorded output to date, the group has already reached cult classic status and shows no signs of abating. This is not an outfit that will make three albums and disappear; it's a refined unit improving with every show and every broken tooth.

Can they keep up their intensity? There's no simple answer to that. True, eventually the fury-laced live shows must abate somewhat – but then, MCR has such an arsenal of inspirations to draw on, and such a talented array of musicians in their number, that they could turn their hand to anything.

Like all the best bands there is always an air of unpredictability to My Chemical Romance, and this – coupled with their utter self-belief and keen intelligence – makes witnessing a live show or hearing a CD an incendiary experience. And a personal one too. Each fan feels as if Gerard is speaking to him or her. Such identity with an audience is a rare thing, especially for a very young band, and it's something MCR will strive to hold on to. For now, everyone is simply happy to be along for the ride. And what a rollercoaster it is proving to be.

ChAPTeR 1

In The
Family

"It's hard to break out of routines there in New Jersey. If I wasn't in this band, I'd probably be stuck doing some retail job. We lived near malls, and that's just what you would do. A lot of people I know ended up as, like, a manager at The Gap." Mikey Way

Gerard Way spilled out into the world on April 9, 1977, in Newark, New Jersey. Born half-Italian (on his mother's side) and half-Scottish (on his father's side), the baby Way arrived at an interesting time for rock music, to say the least. In the same year, EMI famously dropped the Sex Pistols, leaving the door open for Virgin to pick them up and see them become anti-stars; Elvis Presley died of a heart attack aged 42 at his home Graceland in Memphis, Tennessee; and three members of Southern rock legends Lynyrd Skynyrd died in a plane crash. (The tragic accident killed singer and songwriter Ronnie Van Zant, guitarist and vocalist Steve Gaines and vocalist Cassie Gaines not to mention assistant road manager Dean Kilpatrick, and the two pilots.)

Newark – or the Brick City, as it is sometimes called – is the Gateway to New Jersey, the financial, commercial and cultural hub of the Garden State. With the development of the Train-to-Plane system, Newark now boasts one of the most streamlined transportation systems in the world. It had seen its share of drama too, however, not least with race riots in 1967 – after which the city went from having a predominantly middle-class white populace to becoming a relatively poor mixed-race metropolis, seemingly overnight. It would take some thirty years for the city to rejuvenate itself – many saw the emergence of The New Jersey Performing Arts Center, as late as 1997, as a major turning point.

Although New Jersey residents are proud of their state, they are often overshadowed by the looming presence of New York across the water and struggle to stamp their own identity in geographical terms. Perhaps the most famous rock icon from the state of New Jersey is Jon Bon Jovi, though other well-known locals to have become famous include magician David Copperfield, singers Frank Sinatra and Whitney Houston and actor Jack Nicholson.

In fact, show business had already touched the Way family prior to Gerard's birth, courtesy of Joe Rogan (he is Mikey and Gerard's mother's cousin's son). Perhaps a more interesting character than most of the famous Newark residents, Rogan was born on August 11, 1967. His best-known role was as host of the NBC game/stunt show *Fear Factor*, but he is also the commentator for the *Ultimate Fighting Championship*. Joe himself is no slouch in this department, and possesses a black belt in Tae Kwon Do. He was the Massachusetts Full Contact Tae Kwon Do champion four consecutive times, winning it first at the age of nineteen as the lightweight champion. He then went on to beat both the middle- and heavyweight title holders to take home the Grand Championship. As if this wasn't enough, Rogan is also a popular stand-up comedian. Universal good looks seem to be inherent in the genes of the Way family, and ensured that Rogan and the Way brothers would never be short of female interest. With his charismatic good looks, Gerard, in particular, seemed born to perform.

"The most famous Newark natives are rapper Ice-T and the actor Ray Liotta"

The other most famous musician to have emanated from New Jersey is Bruce Springsteen, one of Gerard Way's favourite artists as a youngster. Indeed, the first concert he ever attended (with his mother) was a show by

'The Boss'. Other famous Newark natives are rapper Ice-T and the actor Ray Liotta, but as a young boy Way always felt he had it in him to be famous one day too. He started to learn guitar aged ten, but became frustrated when he found he wasn't progressing as fast as he would have liked, and soon put the instrument to one side. Within a year, Gerard's grandmother gave him his first serious introduction to the musical world. She helped teach him to sing and perform, as well as to draw, and by the age of eleven Gerard was already singing in local bands. "It started really young, with Iron Maiden's Bruce Dickinson," the singer later recalled. "He really inspired me because he's a great front man, a great singer and I've always been influenced by the way he sang."

Gerard may have been destined to be an out-and-out rocker, yet he also exuded a romantic edge even in his younger days. For starters, at one point he became a devoted fan of actress Christina Ricci. Indeed, his fascination was fuelled even further once he realised she lived in New Jersey – stars of that stature are so often LA-based. Ironically, Ricci's paternal grandfather was of Italian descent and the remainder of her ancestry is Scottish, giving her a surprisingly similar lineage to the Ways. It's no surprise Gerard was attracted to Ricci. Besides her cherubic good looks, she exhibited a darker side, whether it be in her acting roles, or simply as an innate characteristic. And in real life, Ricci was reassuringly open, honest and vulnerable. "For years, I hated myself," she has been quoted as saying, "I covered the mirrors in my house. I literally couldn't have a mirror in my room. I still can't sit in a restaurant or some place where I can catch my reflection. I get so paranoid." Although Gerard was never afraid of his own reflection, there were certainly complex issues at play. At a young age he became obsessed with the idea of death and what happens when the body dies. He also felt paranoid that he would lose all those who were close to him and that both he and they would die alone. Gerard read about ouija boards, which did nothing to ease his mind with regards to the possibility of life after death, and the occult. In fact, he found the dark side of life easier to believe and even felt somewhat comforted by its presence.

When Gerard was fifteen he almost gave up on music for good. The band he was playing in at the time allegedly threw him out of the ranks after he would not learn to play Lynyrd Skynyrd's famous song 'Sweet Home Alabama'. So Way turned to his other passion: art. Being a committed connoisseur of comic books, Gerard often took inspiration from familiar comic strips for his drawings, but he also displayed a talent that was all his own – as the My Chemical Romance artwork would later attest. Instead of bumming around on the streets and looking for a new band, Way enrolled in the School of Visual Arts in New York. The SVA, as it is sometimes known, is the largest independent undergraduate art college in the United States, and in 1983 introduced its first graduate offering, a Master of Fine Arts programme in painting, drawing and sculpture.

Whether as part of his own education or not, Gerard did one thing in particular that marked him out from his classmates, as he would later reveal to *Trouble Bunch* magazine. "I went to school in drag, in art school and my day was completely different because everybody thought I was a chick. You should see me as a chick," he joked. "So I went as a girl, as like an experiment and it worked really well and everyone was really nice to me but I couldn't talk obviously... you know train conductors were really cool to me on my commute... HA! I looked hot as a chick!"

Come 1999, Way had graduated with a Bachelor of Fine Arts degree. This almost paid off quickly when he found an intern job at the Cartoon Network. Never content just to be one of the crowd, Gerard had been developing an idea for his own cartoon show. He had named it *The Breakfast Monkey*, and it involved a flying simian who spoke in a similar fashion to eccentric Icelandic singer Björk. The monkey had the ability to make waffles, French toast or any breakfast food appear out of thin air... The official promotional spiel for the cartoon reads: "Positively the most important cartoon of your day, *The Breakfast Monkey* is an edible extravaganza through the wacky world of our squeaky-voiced hero – a monkey with the power of "breakfast magic". His uncanny ability to produce wily waffles and bewitched bacon works wonders in warding off the evil cast of crazy characters of Mod City. Join The Breakfast Monkey and his trusty sidekicks, Crazy Boy and Tinkle Fish, as they try – with good intentions but sometimes disastrous results, to spread good food and good cheer to everyone they meet. Whether they like it or not."

According to Way, an executive at the network was interested in the idea and meetings took place with production companies to discuss licensing deals. However, ultimately his idea was rejected – according to him because it was too similar to *Aqua Teen Hunger Force*, a programme already in production for the network.

"Something just clicked in my head, and that was when I said, 'fuck art'."

Gerard offered an alternative explanation for his change in direction to *Rolling Stone*: "Something just clicked in my head, and that was when I said, 'fuck art' for the first time. I thought, 'Art's not doing anything for you. It's just something on a wall, it's completely disposable, and it's not helping anyone.' And I was like, 'Fuck *Breakfast Monkey*, because all it's gonna do is line somebody else's pockets.' I felt like I had given my life to art and that it had betrayed me. And then I saw Thursday perform at this club for fifty people, and it changed me."

It was in performing that Gerard Way truly discovered himself. Although he had the raw talent in his very early teens, and his grandmother helped perfect his singing style, he had never truly longed for a career as a vocalist – until Thursday changed his mind. Formed in New Brunswick, New Jersey in 1997, Thursday are generally considered a hardcore group, though they are one of the lucky ones to have traversed the fine line between hardcore and emo. As front man Geoff Rickly says, "I consider ourselves a hardcore band. A lot of people will say that we're a emo band or whatever. I just think that's a really dumb label. If music doesn't have emotion in it, then it's not really music. Everything I listen to has emotion in it. I listen to Dave Matthews and I feel that has a lot of emotion in it. I listen to Grade. I listen to most heavy bands. I listen to You And I, and that has a lot of emotion in it. For us, I still consider ourselves a hardcore band even though a lot of people consider us a pop band." Thursday released their debut, *Waiting*, in 1999 through the New York-based independent label Eyeball, but they were soon snapped up by Chicago's legendary (and heavily hardcore) Victory label for their 2001 opus *Full Collapse*.

> *"I've been a fan of music and I've always wanted to be in a band. I just never had the urge to be a front man until I saw him do it."*

Not only was Gerard Way aware of Thursday because they were a local band (he would later go on to design some of their merchandise), he also found inspiration in the music itself – and specifically in the performances of vocalist Rickly. "Geoff from Thursday inspired me as a person to just get up and be a lead singer," Way acknowledged to *Metal Underground*. "I've been a fan of music and I've always wanted to be in a band. I just never had the urge to be a front man until I saw him do it. I was like, 'You know what? It just seems so incredible and it seems like he's actually making a difference and he was doing something.' Right at that moment is when I knew I would do it."

Meeting Rickly face to face was also inspirational in its own way. "I met Geoff outside a record store called St Marks in Kearny," Gerard told *Alternative Press*, "and he was this really strange-looking kid who looked like he was in Joy Division. He had a black mop, looked emaciated and pale-as-shit sick. But he was so nice and we hit it off immediately." For his part, Geoff Rickly remembers Way as someone who was more than a little enigmatic himself. The two would often bump into each other at parties thrown by Eyeball Records, organised by label owner Alex Saavedra. "When you'd see him he would look terrible, just bummed out," Rickly remarked to *Alternative Press* of Way. "He told me one night that Thursday gave him new hope and he was gonna start a band with his little brother. Not that it was a joke, but I thought, 'Yeah they're thinking about starting a band but how long does it take before they start something good?' He would sit there and play me songs on one of Alex's guitars that was so hopelessly out of tune and broken with bad strings that I couldn't even tell what he was doing. But I was like, 'I love you and your brother and sure, I'll hang out and come to practice.'"

Comics had, of course, always formed an important part of Gerard's life. As an artist he was mostly in love with the art form and appearance of comics, but equally took heart from superheroes in many stories, from Superman to Spiderman, not to mention being inspired by romantic connotations within many of the comics he would read. Little did he know he would soon be able to combine his love of art and music to a spectacular and successful degree.

The earth-shattering political events of the most significant date in US history for many decades – the date when the financial twin towers in New York were hit by terrorist attacks and almost 3,000 people were killed – had an immediate effect on the young Way's own life: "9/11 happened and literally a week later the phone calls were made," Gerard would say on the subject of his life-changing move. The year 2001 was perhaps a fateful year for My Chemical Romance to come together. It had started with the controversial appointment of George W Bush Jr as the President of the United States and after the democrat Bill Clinton had presided mostly successfully over the world's most powerful nation for eight years, the country was now in the hands of a Republican. In the United Kingdom, a second term for Labour leader Tony Blair was underway, with millions around the globe unaware of the chaos the union of Bush and Blair would eventually bring to the world. The terrorist attacks on New York affected Way deeply – unsurprisingly so, given that he lived in the next state. It may have seemed at the time as if the world was beginning to fall apart, but there was a way to kick against the pricks, the age-old way, the thing you just

'did' when nothing else would work: you formed a band. Way met up with Matt Pelissier at the Loop Lounge in Passaic, New Jersey, and there the two effectively began the story of My Chemical Romance. "I ran into Matt and I said, 'You know what? I've been writing songs. I'm not doing anything, you're not doing anything, so let's get together and give it a shot.'" Way also played the drummer a rough version of 'Skylines And Turnstiles' and the latter was buoyed by what he heard.

As with many bands, My Chemical Romance was not to be the first group most of its members had ever played in. Indeed, throughout their teenage years, the individuals had passed through a succession of bands that were perennially struggling – though it was all good experience. The original line-up of MCR would come together later in 2001, when Gerard Way decided to form an outfit that took inspiration from his heroes – namely Iron Maiden, Green Day and David Bowie. The name My Chemical Romance came from the Irvine Welsh novel *Three Tales Of Chemical Romance*. Many of Welsh's works came under the category 'chemical romances', as the young characters in the books were often hooked on drugs and/or alcohol. And then there were the romances between the characters themselves. Needless to say, such a name also courted controversy and the members of MCR would later be regularly asked to confirm that they didn't endorse narcotic indulgence.

Something about the manner in which Gerard Way went about forming the nucleus of a rock group recalls the famous occasion when Jim Morrison mooted the idea of forming a band called The Doors to his UCLA film school buddy Ray Manzarek. As would later be immortalised in Oliver Stone's movie *The Doors*, on the beach at Venice, California, one day Morrison sang to Manzarek the lyrics he had for a song, 'Moonlight Drive'. Manzarek was impressed, but was then simply bowled over when he realised Morrison had the full concept of the band planned out in his head already. From such a simple gathering one afternoon quietly on the Californian sand a great union was forged, with The Doors eventually going on to become one of the biggest rock acts of all time, perfectly in line with Morrison's original vision. Gerard Way was of the same stock, a man assured of his role in a group he knew would be able to change at least some small part of the world. His chance meeting with Matt Pelissier was to be fateful for both men, and the seeds of My Chemical Romance were sown.

However, Gerard was still learning to simultaneously sing and play guitar, so it was never going to work unless the band could find at least one guitarist. Pelissier had previously been in a band with Ray Toro, and Gerard rang him the same night, telling him, "No strings attached, you don't have to say yes or no. Just come, check it out and bring your guitar."

"There was this guy who was this drug addict. Every couple of weeks he would OD outside my house."

Raymond Toro Ortiz was born July 15, 1977, in Newark, New Jersey. He lived on a dead-end street on the border of Kearny and Harrison where he grew up as a member of a Puerto Rican household. "There was definitely a funny collection of people hanging round my block," the guitarist told *Alternative Press*. "There was this guy who was this drug addict. Every couple of weeks he would OD outside my house. I would see an ambulance come and take him away." Though he attended the same high school as Gerard and Mikey, Ray would later claim they were merely 'loose friends'. He reconnected with Gerard at an Iron Maiden show and it was here they hatched a plan to create a band that would dwarf all others in the alternative rock scene. They had a name, and they now had the beginnings of a band, with Ortiz as the chief songwriter and the strongest musical composer of the four. In fact, when MCR recruited their final jigsaw piece, it would be Ortiz who would take the younger Frank Iero on board most quickly.

Frank Anthony Iero (pronounced 'eye-year-oh') was born on October 31, 1981, in Belleville, New Jersey. Iero is a proud native of NJ and has been quoted as saying he prefers living there to New York or Los Angeles, as it has a more communal feel. Iero did not settle too well at school – he was often bullied and at only 5'4" was always going to find larger boys unfairly advantaged. Another band member blessed with good looks, with his hazel eyes and dark-brown natural hair (which he now dyes black), Iero was the archetypal short kid sometimes picked on at school. Perhaps in part due to his harsh treatment by fellow children, he was often in and out of hospital as a child; he suffered from several ear infections and also bronchitis.

"There were times when we really couldn't even afford milk."

The fact his parents had also divorced when he was very young exacerbated his childhood stresses. Frank grew up with his mother, though he retained contact with a father whom he cites as being a great influence.

"My parents split up when I was pretty young," Iero would later tell *Alternative Press*. "There were times when we really couldn't even afford milk. But I wouldn't change my upbringing for the world." (aping the admirable attitude of Green Day)

Leaving high school, Iero went on to attend Rutgers University for four years. However he dropped out, and also left a band he was in at the time called Pencey Prep, when approached by Gerard Way to join My Chemical Romance, who needed a second guitarist to bolster their sound. Pencey Prep were already well known by the Way brothers, given they were signed to Eyeball. Moreover, Thursday, Pencey Prep and the origins of My Chemical Romance would all use the same rehearsal space. Gerard's kid brother Mikey Way (who would soon join the band) would later explain to *Alternative Press*: "We would all practise in the same room, which was great because you could just hang out, watch someone else's practice, do your own, share ideas, and show people what was going on. It was awesome."

Come September, the five guys were proficient enough to record a demo in Pelissier's attic. "My attic had no walls," the drummer explained to *Alternative Press*. "It was a wooden run-down piece of crap. I had a really cheap 16-track board, and we had a bunch of crappy mics. I basically had the drums and guitars playing upstairs and ran the mics downstairs and had Gerard sing in the bathroom." The sessions produced early versions of tracks that were to appear on the very first My Chemical Romance album. These included

'Cubicles', 'Skylines And Turnstiles' and 'Our Lady Of Sorrows', which was initially titled 'Bring More Knives'. The rudimentary demo made an immediate impact on almost all those who heard it, as Gerard remembers: "You could hear that it was something really new, and it was kind of a weird idea, but for some reason, as poorly as it was coming together, it really worked."

ChAPteR 2

Not Of This World

"When I was writing, I was remembering how hard it was to be a sixteen-year-old in high school. I always wanted to be an artist, so I was this loner kid who just got drunk all the time. I only had one real friend. There was a girl I really liked, and she ended up taking really sleazy photographs with her boyfriend, and that really crushed me, I was just swimming in this pit of despair."

Gerard Way

The three-song demo My Chemical Romance recorded proved to Gerard's little brother Mikey that this was a serious project for the singer. And for Gerard, no one would be more suitable as a bass player than his younger brother Mikey. Born Michael

James Way, on September 10, 1980, also in Newark, Mikey was always blessed with a close relationship with his older sibling and this led to a perfect coupling for the band.

> *"From the theatric intro to the thundering choruses, what else could you want in rock and roll? I was sold…"*

As a teenager, Mikey and Gerard had both held a number of temporary low-wage jobs (their parents, Donna and Donald, are a former hairdresser and an auto-dealer service manager, respectively), including shelving books at a Barnes & Noble store, shelving peas and in the frozen-foods section at a local supermarket. But Mikey's most significant early job was that of an intern at Eyeball Records. It gave him a working knowledge of the music business, as well as a chance to develop friendships and business contacts through the label, all of which would prove very useful later on. The first concert Mikey attended was a Smashing Pumpkins show but it was a particular live record that really set the scene for him to start playing music, as he recalled to *Teen Spot*: "I could pinpoint the live album by Iron Maiden, *Live After Death*, as the catalyst for me wanting to play music. From the theatric intro to the thundering choruses, what else could you want in rock and roll? I was sold…"

He may have been ready to rock at the drop of a hat, but Mikey was hardly the typical rock star. He is near-sighted and suffers from asthma, though he does smoke and has experienced upper respiratory problems. Not ideal when you are on the road constantly. Yet nothing would stop him joining a band with his brother, and he dropped out of college to learn bass and join Gerard in My Chemical Romance. As the two would later explain in many interviews, there were several advantages to being brothers in a band, especially as far as touring went. The best thing was that they knew each other inside out, and though Gerard was slightly older, they had many things in common.

Most importantly they could tolerate each other's behaviour; each would know when the other was tired, angry, upset or happy. The two of them knew when to come up and say 'hi', when to embrace and when to stay the fuck away, without even having to talk to each other. "When you're in a band it takes a while to become brothers with the other guys, but you eventually do," said Gerard to *The Punk Site* of his other eventual band mates. "But it definitely makes it easier because you know you have at least one person that you've lived with so long, that you get along with so well that you can kind of go out and go shopping for comics or something, whatever. But, it's not really that way in this band where we need to get away from each other. We all get along extremely well, like brothers, and we all do the same things, we all play video games and we go out comic shopping with each other."

Whether it was due to his contacts at Eyeball, or simply to the fact Eyeball got to hear the band first and knew they would be huge, it was the label MCR were all most familiar with who signed them first. It was probably a good thing there was already a label who knew of their work, as My Chemical Romance were hardly self-promoters. "We kind of anti-promoted. We would play shows and not say our name," Gerard Way told *Pollstar*. "We didn't make stickers, we didn't have merchandise. The first thing we had was a website. I just felt like we were doing this for a reason." This anti-promotion probably fuelled greater interest anyway – whispers and hearsay can be far more effective than straightforward mass marketing. Brian Schechter – of management company Riot Squad – was working as a tour manager when he first heard MCR's demo. It changed his life instantly. "I always listened to every demo the bands I used to tour with would get," Schechter informed *Pollstar*. "I knew right when I heard it that if there was a band I was going to stop touring and put everything I had in to, it was My Chemical Romance."

No one could tell from watching, but Mikey Way was extremely nervous, more so than any other member, during his first few gigs with the band, and would often consume lots of alcohol to mask his stage fright. Yet play he did, and the early MCR shows were vital building blocks for the fearsome live reputation they were to gain – and all created with minimum promotion. Effectively, the band itself was the promotion: all anyone needed was to simply see a show and they'd be sure to spread the MCR gospel by word of mouth thereafter. The best and most consistently successful bands tend to be talked about for a while before exploding, and My Chemical Romance were no exception. But first they needed a record with which to sell their wares. They already had the material; the key now was to transfer the feral angst of their live shows onto disc. It wasn't going to be easy, but already plans were being made to go beyond a demo. Somewhat unusually, MCR would not need more than one demo before they were ready to record their first full-length album; their competence and attitude were already assured.

"He was overwhelmed and he was overthinking it. So I punched him in the face!"

In early 2002 the band booked into Nada Studios in New York, with Geoff Rickly and Alex Saavedra coming along for moral support. The sessions were hit by torrential rainstorms and affected by ill health, but out of the carnage emerged the debut album *I Brought You My Bullets, You Brought Me Your Love.* Saavedra recalled in *Alternative Press*, "As soon as it came time for Gerard to do 'Vampires (Will Never Hurt You)' this insane storm hit. He was getting very frustrated because it was his first time recording decently, in an actual studio. He was overwhelmed and

he was overthinking it. So I punched him in the face!" Something other than mere flesh connected, and Gerard's loose jaw managed to tighten his act, enabling him to cut a remarkable vocal performance in the process. "I remember it hurting a lot," Gerard responded in the same magazine, "I thought, 'All right, I hope I can do this.' I remember singing and something clicked and Alex's face was just amazed that something was coming together. I think it was the second take that we ended up using."

The record was finished in just under two weeks and was instantly a hit with anyone who heard it. Though the transfer from demo to live shows to first album had been fast, a considerable amount of thought had already gone into MCR's overall game plan – lyrics included. As Gerard Way would testify, "Before the record, I said to myself, 'Man, I'm so tired of hearing songs about people's ex-girlfriends. It's really nauseating. And the whole 'me, me, me' aspect of it was just overdone." Most likely Way was referring to the emo mentality of many bands – emo being the cry-baby genre of modern soft rock, in which songs typically wallowed in layers of pain and suffering only a grunge band from Seattle could truly understand. Yet whereas those bands who drew on this former genre in the Nineties – such as Alice In Chains, Pearl Jam and Soundgarden et al – produced mostly excellent bodies of work, the more modern form of the "me, me, me" mentality was doused with saccharine, bland pop, with barely a hint of a chorus. Many of these bands dominated the alternative scene in 2001, and most weren't worthy of a place alongside the accomplished bands of the Nineties.

Gerard didn't care for that other scourge of the previous decade either – the abomination known as nu-metal. Korn, Limp Bizkit and Linkin Park were MTV babies and they had inspired an abundance of weak and tame imitators who were desperate for money and fame, rather than literally feeling the music and playing because it was inherent. My Chemical Romance were different and everyone who heard them knew it, including the band. "We knew what we had was very kind of new, and very exciting and very inventive," Gerard told *City Beat*. "It still needed to be banged into shape, we thought. The first record is a band discovering who it is, we were only three months in as a band so we were still trying to figure out who we were."

Nevertheless, *I Brought You My Bullets You Brought Me Your Love* is a remarkable debut album. Unlike so many other alternative rock acts, who burst out of nowhere – only to fade even more quickly – My Chemical Romance had almost reinvented the wheel – though for some lazy journalists it was too easy to compare the album to work by one of the group's closest musical allies, Thursday. Despite both bands being from New Jersey, both being on Eyeball Records and Geoff Rickly producing the album, the sound was still a world apart. In a tremendously short time, MCR had raised the bar for even their best friends.

"We were the most different band in Jersey at the time."

Interestingly, though MCR's contemporaries such as Jimmy Eat World, Yellowcard, Taking Back Sunday and Matchbook Romance are listed on emo pages on the internet, My Chemical Romance's name rarely gets a mention alongside them. And only rarely do they crop up in connection with gothic acts such as Type O Negative and Nightwish, though it's possible to see some similarities between MCR and Finland's HIM. Put simply, My Chemical Romance are beyond emo, screamo, alternative, goth, punk and heavy metal. But though there are more musical genres around in the

21st century than ever before, it is a testament to MCR that they can neatly sidestep any specific brand of rock. Reviews of *I Brought You My Bullets, You Brought Me Your Love* were sparkling in their enthusiasm. *Metal Hammer* gushed, "A hard hitting punk rock explosion – incredible." *Kerrang!* exclaimed, "Astonishing – they're going to be huge." *Rocksound* avoided pigeonholing the group, despite the obvious connotations of the magazine's readership, when they boldly stated, "My Chemical Romance are without exception, what every band should sound like, buy now!"

It was inevitable that the rock-oriented magazines would appreciate MCR, as for every snippet of influence from The Cure or The Smiths there is also a strong undercurrent of unashamedly metal bands like Iron Maiden and straightforward punks such as The Misfits. Gerard Way, for one, was certainly not about to jump on the emo bandwagon, commenting to *Designer* magazine, "We were, like, please, this emo shit has got to stop. We were called emo originally because we were a product of our environment. If you'd kinda been from Jersey at the time you'd realise that we were the most different band in Jersey at the time. I just hope that whatever we do it's classified as rock."

Gerard would further expand upon his band's exact style to *The Punk Site*: "This is probably every band's answer, but we really categorise ourselves as a rock and roll band. I always like to use the term 'neo death' to describe it because it's kind of like this new wave of death rock, which is a genre but I feel like that's just a part of us, to be a death rock band. All of our stuff's about death and I don't see that really changing. I mean, it's positive too; it's very positive music. It looks at death in both the negative and positive aspect." In truth, My Chemical Romance were hardly likely to be lumped into the death-metal category, given their comparatively tame sound, and their heartfelt, introspective lyrics. True death metal involves speedy time signatures, double bass drums and often unintelligible growling and grunting – but death rock, that was something else entirely. Death rock seemed glamorous, yet was ultimately a morose genre probably most appropriate for those shoe-gazers who existed on the periphery, outside the circles of the more popular high-school kids.

The term death rock was first coined in the Fifties, after Jody Reynolds performed a song called 'Endless Sleep', and the first wave is often said to have ended in 1964 with J. Frank Wilson's 'The Last Kiss' (which was covered beautifully by Pearl Jam in 1999). Perhaps the most famous song to arise from the initial movement was The Shangri-La's 'Leader Of The Pack', which though upbeat musically featured an undeniably grim lyric. The characters who populated death-rock songs were loved ones who died from illness or suicide. Although the first series of death-rock groups and performers soon faded, come the end of the Seventies, the term was revitalised when a band called Christian Death hit the punk scene. The name was a morbid take on the moniker of the designer Christian Dior and featured in its ranks one Rozz Williams. This enigmatic front man was born Roger Alan Painter in Pomona, California, but in consummate gothic fashion took his pseudonym from a gravestone in his local cemetery. Like Gerard Way, Williams took inspiration from the likes of David Bowie and Alice Cooper, half mimicking their individual personalities while stamping his own authority all over his band's music. On April 1, 1998, Rozz Williams was found by his roommate, Ryan, hanged in their West Hollywood apartment; he was 34. The irony that one of death rock's leading lights had committed suicide was not lost on Gerard Way.

Way's other favourites, The Misfits, took the death rock tag one step further with their ugly brand of death rock and punk. Although they would later properly develop their deathly sentiments and ghoulish stage attire, it was a line in one of their first songs that gave them some credit for being at the helm of the second wave of death rock. Their 1979 song 'All Hell Breaks Loose' featured the lyric, "and broken bodies in a death rock dance hall". This may well have been simply a cool-sounding line to use, yet many listeners picked up on the term and death rock received another new lease of life. Rozz Williams and Christian Death moved in one direction – sombre, eloquent gothic poetry set to music; The Misfits moved in another, playing fast and to-the-point punk hymns, the likes of which represented macabre humour at its blackest. No doubt this is one of the reasons Gerard and his MCR band mates were inspired by the group. Since leaving The Misfits', original front man Glenn Danzig has made a long career out of combining the rock 'n' roll lineage of Elvis Presley and Roy Orbison with modern-day hard rock.

Death rock has always been a serious business and suits My Chemical Romance perfectly. The music world can merely hope their legacy is longer-lasting than the lives of so many of their heroes.

ChAPteR 3

Unleash the Bats

"That's what happens when you're all borderline psychotic, and therein lies the beauty of this band – our duality. There's a duality to each band member too. There's a desire to have this constant conflict. If we write a write a song and it turns out really poppy, we have to make the lyrics really fucked up. There's psychosis to everything we do for sure. One day we're probably gonna write this Number 1 pop tune that will be about a massacre!" Gerard Way

"I heard 'Vampires (Will Never Hurt You),' on a college radio station and it was probably the biggest thing to me in the world. I think it had, like, a hundred-mile radius." You can almost hear the wonder in his voice as Gerard Way spoke to *Florida*

Entertainment Scene website of the first time he realised My Chemical Romance were actually getting somewhere. It was a small step, but one the band felt would lead further – and quickly too. *I Brought You My Bullets, You Brought Me Your Love* is a resolutely dark album, both musically and lyrically. The artwork within the CD booklet is black and white, portraying the band as a group of sombre individuals with a maelstrom of emotion within. This was not exactly intended, though neither was it an act, but it served MCR well. Here was the type of group that only drops into a record company's hands once every ten years. A collection of perfectly shaped individuals who rose above any personal mental hardship in order to bring a selection of heartfelt, identifiable music to all the misfits and outcasts of the world. The bullied child at school now had a band who understood his problems, who could almost be playing just for him. The process of making the record had certainly not been an easy one: Gerard Way was quoted as saying that the band's lyrics were a great way for him to deal with the problems he had been going through of late (which unfortunately included a serious illness in his family). He also suffered from an abscess in his mouth throughout the recording of the album, which added a nagging physical discomfort to mental unease.

The first MCR album is not as well produced as their follow-up recording, yet it buzzes with intense energy from the moment 'Romance' starts up, with a novel acoustic guitar pattern and series of samples. 'Honey

This Mirror Isn't Big Enough For The Two Of Us' kicks in with a stirring guitar riff that betrayed the distinctive influence of Iron Maiden – in particular, Maiden's swashbuckling classic 'Flash Of The Blade', from their 1984 *Powerslave* album. Within the opening few minutes, all the multiple facets of the band members' listening tastes had converged to create a neat encapsulation of the beast that was My Chemical Romance. Within the confines of a rousing first song proper the listener was exposed to Gerard's tortured howl, and every musical genre from screamo, to indie and back again via pop and heavy metal. 'Honey...' featured lines that were perhaps a deliberate snipe at the emo tag MCR were so desperate to avoid? Yet there were very real cries of anger throughout the song, which was about an ex-girlfriend of Gerard's. At gigs he would often 'dedicate' the song to his ex – by saying, "This song is about a big fat whore." And who said the ultimate compliment was having a song written about you? The searing emotion of this song was to typify much of Gerard's lyrical slant.

After such a cathartic opening drive, it was time for a typical gothic paean – or at least so it seemed on the first listen – 'Vampires (Will Never Hurt You)'. Mention corpses, venom, spikes in the heart and razor-sharp white teeth and thousands of eyeliner-bedaubed devotees will be yours... Yet it stands up equally as a depiction of those living on the outskirts of mainstream society – such as gothic rock fans. The lyrics could well be a metaphor for avoiding people who seek to destroy those who are living their lives freely, an attack on individuals who contribute nothing to anything outside themselves – and who therefore might as well be corpses. Too many so-called 'normal' people really seem dead on the inside, yet the irony is that 'alternative' rockers are often viewed as some sort of children of the devil. "Yeah, obviously we use vampires as a metaphor for something else," Gerard confirmed, "something deeper than just the supernatural. But there's just something about the bloodsucking walking dead that can say so much to people. There are really so many people trying to get control over you on a daily basis and steal your soul in some way, take a part of you..."

'Drowning Lessons' provides another good metaphor, for highlighting the way some people can never be broken – instead of drowning and dying, they learn how to cope with being proverbially pushed under water time and time again. For some, this kind of reference seemed too negative; there are even those who claimed (wrongly) that the band were promoting suicide in the song. Gerard would frequently be asked about his lyrics in interviews, and repeatedly he had to explain the My Chemical Romance stance on songs such as 'Drowning Lessons', a track that was actually about a relationship going nowhere. Even boy bands could identify with the sentiment expressed here, though perhaps they might not be able to bring themselves to tackle the same subject with lyrics concerning cheap champagne and laughing as you die. This was hardly the domain of The Backstreet Boys.

"We are a very anti-suicide band," Gerard Way told *Crush Music* magazine, "because we have been dealing with mental depression all our lives. I mean, everyone gets depressed but so few people address depression in music. And that's always just been one of our messages, because so few people address what's wrong with them and communicate their problems. And we also like to be very accepting of all kinds of people. We like to be different from other hardcore bands by riding the line between homosexuality and heterosexuality just to push buttons and [raise] awareness. One of the greatest things about our shows, when you look out there, is that you find a lot of kids that don't match each other at all. It's not like a scene show and that's the way we love it."

'Our Lady Of Sorrows' was a rallying cry for all those who felt different to embrace their fellow outsiders. Quite often, Gerard would introduce the song live with a friendly stage rant: "You probably came with your best friend, or one of your best friends... I want you to turn to that motherfucker, grab him by the throat and say, 'You're my best fucking friend, and I would die for you!'" Way was serious as a heart attack, too. He would reveal to *Concert Live Wire*, "My favourite lyrics are from 'Our Lady of Sorrows'. I can't imagine I'm going to top that. I don't think I will *try*. I mean, it says a lot to me. Says a lot about how we felt about the band in the beginning..." So, although the words are about sticking together with your friends, they are also a reference to the inner sanctum of My Chemical Romance.

"You're my best fucking friend, and I would die for you!"

Lyrics from this track are symptomatic of MCR's appeal, offering a helping hand that would save several teenagers from taking their own life (Gerard's habit of meeting fans after each show at the First Aid desk was a more specific example of the genuine help and support his band and their music offered thousands). It was as if they were being directly addressed by the vocalist and he alone could save them – like a kind of superhero, in fact.

'Headfirst For Halos' comes across as a somewhat odd track in the middle of a set of brusque, battle-ready numbers. This could almost have been a song from an Offspring record, with an upbeat riff highly reminiscent of the poppy hardcore outfit – not something one would generally associate with MCR. Of course, with Gerard's impassioned vo-kills, the riff was generally overshadowed. The contrast was deliberate, though: the voice sounded angry and hurt, but the 'poppy' riff masked the lyrics' downbeat tone.

Next up was the song that started it all, 'Skylines And Turnstiles'. In truth, it was not the strongest track on the album, and was certainly an indication that My Chemical Romance was not yet quite the finished article. In fairness to the band, this was something they themselves acknowledged. As Gerard would observe to *The Punk Site*, "we weren't super huge fans of a lot of the songs on that record and we knew what we could improve. I mean, we were only a band for three months when we made it and all the songs that are on that record are the only songs that we had. We literally squeezed every one we could out of ourselves to make that record." More of a diehard early fans' song, 'Skylines And Turnstiles' struggled to find a gripping chorus, though it still possessed an inherent charm, especially towards the end, with words about reclaiming innocence and defying the world, regular MCR themes. Despite the track's flaws, it became a highly significant part of the MCR pantheon, and not simply because it was the first song Gerard presented to the band when they first formed. The lyrics deal with Way's feelings after the horror of September 11, 2001. Unlike many bands,

MCR were in the unique position of not only being extremely close to the area of the tragedy (Gerard was at the Cartoon Network offices at the time and witnessed the whole thing), but also of having had the drive and energy to compose a song about the events almost immediately after they occurred. Some bands were in the unfortunate position of penning a song about the attacks, only to have to wait three or four years for it to hit the record stores. MCR were able to articulate an altogether more immediate sense of loss and confusion – and were blessed with better timing – than many other groups, who would simply jump on the bandwagon of either criticising President George Bush or, conversely, speaking out on behalf of American conservatism à la Billy Milano, of MOD and SOD fame.

Gerard Way inadvertently set himself up as something of a potential martyr with the gripping and harrowing track 'Early Sunsets Over Monroeville'. Towards the end of the song, Way is audibly distressed, sounding like a young Henry Rollins on a very bad day. It makes for uncomfortable listening, as if the listener were privy to an area of the singer's life that should never have been revealed in public. But for anyone assuming the lyrics might be hinting at morose thoughts or depression, the vocalist lightened the load by claiming in interviews it was a song about the movie *Dawn Of The Dead*.

The urgency of My Chemical Romance's first album was evident for all to hear – "A big obnoxious sounding rock record. There was this feeling of bringing a real rock band back," Gerard told *Designer* – something that was certainly evident on tracks such as 'This Is The Best Day Ever'. "Even when you see us live it sounds as if there's ten guitarists up on stage 'cos Frank and Ray have so much going on and complement each other so well," continued Gerard. It was certainly evident in the guitar overload of this particular track. Frank picked out scintillating riffs that played right under what Gerard was singing, while Ray blasted out great big power chords. Although later more complex albums may see attitudes change, for now MCR are a band who write songs with the live show in mind, which ensures that the incendiary energy of their gigs is easily transferred on to each record.

'This Is The Best Day Ever' was a song perfect for a live setting; though its mood was traumatic – dare I say, almost emo – it was also one of the best tracks on the album. The lyrics referred to several stays in the hospital that Way made while making the album due to ill health, the title asserting how happy he would be to leave the place for good.

'Cubicles' was a particularly catchy track, and although it was the penultimate song on the album it was sure to maintain the listener's attention, which was of crucial importance for a debut record. The song was a variation on the romantic theme, a lyrical wail for approval from a girl Gerard liked (whether for real or for the sake of a song is not known) but who seemed unaware he even existed. As the singer wept about the sadness of dying alone, he was fuelling the fire

for more emo comparisons, but it was undeniably a strong track.

Gerard whispers about ending his and his lover's days in a hail of bullets on the final track of MCR's debut offering, 'Demolition Lovers'. Part of an ambitious trilogy, which would later be expanded upon with the group's second album, track 11 is in part a homage to Quentin Tarantino's *Natural Born Killers* movie. The film focused on two characters, Mickey and Mallory Knox (played by Woody Harrelson and Juliette Lewis respectively). The tagline for the "ambitious new film" was "The Media Made Them Superstars". The plot focused on the two lovers who, despite their ongoing desire to kill, were incredibly in love and would do anything for each other. The script revolved around the media's appetite for fame and crime (just look at how many American shows follow cops on duty, or people going wild being chased by them). *Natural Born Killers*, it seemed, was a film made just for someone like Gerard Way to draw inspiration from.

In Way's adaptation of this theme, the two characters are both killed and sent to purgatory. The male will only be able to reach his partner again if he kills a thousand evil men. 'Demolition Lovers' is the story of how the two died, though 'Drowning Lessons' also references the demolition lovers trilogy with a line about 1,000 bodies piled up. As with most of MCR's material, however, ordinary real-life emotions surface too – pain, heartache and, more rarely, contentment. It seems Gerard wrote 'Demolition Lovers' with a particular person in mind as he mentions the final song on the album in the inner-sleeve liner notes, "To K: I'm sorry I write all these songs about killing you, I hope the last track makes up for it."

Overall, *I Brought You My Bullets, You Brought Me Your Love* may have been the record that got My Chemical Romance noticed in the alternative music world, but it was their subsequent live performances and clever promotion of the album that would spur the band on to worldwide attention and greatness. As the sleeve artwork suggested, and the back inner sleeve stated, it really was time to unleash the bats!

ChAPteR 4

Bring Me
Your Love

*"Playing live erases everything I hate about myself.
Nothing can hurt me. I feel completely invincible.
I feel like everyone else on that stage is invincible
and we're capable of anything. There's no stopping us."*
                                                    Gerard Way

The first serious batch of touring My Chemical
Romance engaged in was to follow the release of
*I Brought You My Bullets, You Brought Me Your
Love*. It brought the band closer to their potential, and
naturally, to their growing fan base, but also toughened
the members up very quickly and showed them proof, if
any were needed, that rock 'n' roll was as boring as it

was glamorous. Endless days spent waiting to go onstage, being in cities they had never heard of; sometimes they didn't even know *where* they were.

"It was a total crash course and we never stopped touring..."

"I'll definitely say that we got a crash course very quickly in it and the amount of sickness and turmoil that we went through in that two and half years probably equals about six years," Gerard would later admit to *Crush Music*, with the weariness of a road veteran. "It was a total crash course and we never stopped touring... and financially we couldn't really keep up so we'd just have to eat shit. We just kept doing these tours and it got to the point where we couldn't even afford hotel rooms even though we were on these big tours." It would be some time before the band's global success filtered through to improve tour circumstances.

MCR took it upon themselves to provide a brutal, theatrical experience rather than a straightforward gig (one observer described them on stage as being like "a swarm of vampire bats"). Their early live shows were often vicious experiences, during which band members would fight with each other onstage, trash their instruments and spit in each other's faces. "We just went out there and tried to destroy things," says Gerard. "I didn't want people to stand there and look at it like it was art. We wanted it to be explosive and cathartic."

The first real interest in the band had been stirred up with that vivid, bubbly explosion of a debut album. The studio doesn't lie: what you put in is generally what you get back, and as long as the producer is able, a band is on show for the world to see when releasing any product. Luckily, *I Brought You My Bullets, You Brought Me Your Love* was a good one and it brought the band attention from numerous major labels, all aching to be the one who cottoned on to the next big thing first. Of course, it was really Eyeball's vision that had helped make a success out of My Chemical Romance. Out of all the majors vying for the MCR signatures, one stood out as being *the* one who understood the band best. Coming from an underground scene, bands are always discovering just how little the 'suits' in their tinsel towers truly appreciate their sound, let alone their way of life. Yet, for MCR, Warners/Reprise Records seemed to 'get it'.

What they would also get, however, was a singer with a fairly chaotic lifestyle. For the band's two-year period of touring, Gerard Way was drinking before and after many shows. If anything, it probably fuelled the vocalist's fire, and My Chemical Romance's gigs were all the better for it. However, personally Way was toiling in some areas, a fact not helped by living on the road – in fact, he would list "liver damage" as one of his ailments on the band's official website (he is never one to try to hide away).

Gerard certainly wasn't the first rock star to enjoy a drink on the road – after all, even at a high level, touring can be an exhausting and at times mind-numbing experience. Gerard's tendency to have a drink was merely a side issue for the first real tour MCR had undertaken, though: their musical world was moving like a whirlwind, and what would most 25-year-old guys on the road do but drink to pass the time? Of course, other members had their share of alcohol and enjoyed partying too. As Gerard once said, reflecting back on his high-school days, "I was this weird loner kid who got drunk by himself all the time." For the moment however, the band was able to keep tight as a unit, playing superb shows wherever they went. And during off time they were busy composing the material for their sophomore album.

All the members knew exactly what they wanted to achieve with their next record, and they felt with a better budget and an invigorated sense of what their public wanted they could achieve it, and blow *I Brought You My Bullets, You Brought Me Your Love* out of the water. "The first album was really a good example of a band that wanted to tour a lot and play live," Gerard told *Designer*. "So our concern was just getting something out so the kids could learn the lyrics, sing along with us to our favourite songs and really understand what the band was about." MCR had, after all, only been a band three months when they recorded that debut album. They have since said that they'd wished they'd sent more time capturing that first record, yet they also strongly champion the record as a snapshot of their frantic lives at the time. Far better that a new band ploughs into the studio and somehow captures the very essence of the songs which have made them popular enough to warrant recording an album, than to over-think a debut record and produce something more suitable to AOR radio or a dinosaur rock act.

Besides, the thought that the debut was an example of a band *not* firing on all cylinders, meant a daunting proposition for the follow-up. From Eyeball Records' staff to Warners folks, though – and all MCR fans besides – everyone knew that the best was yet to come. Inevitably, with such expectation came pressure. My Chemical Romance was now an established band for their legions of growing fans and their next recording was hotly awaited. The group felt the weight of anticipation, but dealt with it as they had dealt with everything in their short career to date – with a shrug of the shoulders and a collective mantra: we can only do our best.

Gerard acknowledged to *The Punk Site* that, "Basically, we knew there was going to be a lot of pressure because the first record kind of got a lot of critical attention but at the same time we realised that not many people had heard it. So we kind of had that on our side. We didn't let the pressure of making a good first record get to us and this time we had a lot more time to think about stuff and it was way easier, there were songs that didn't make this record and it was cool to have stuff to choose from." Indeed, where on the debut, everything the group had was immortalised on plastic, by virtue of the fact they hadn't been around long enough to amass a huge catalogue, now they had more material than they would need for the next album that would eventually comprise thirteen songs.

The band members also found themselves under pressure in the form of the inevitable cries that they had 'sold out' by signing to a major label. But as part of MCR's acceptance of the Warners strategy they were rewarded with an allowance to do things their own way. "A lot of people see signing with a major label making a deal with the devil," said Gerard in answer to these tiresome accusations. "But the funny thing is that they left us alone entirely and let us do our own thing so it's kinda the opposite… they've been incredible with us."

In fact, the freedom which Warners gave to MCR is probably far more generous than many independent labels could boast. The band made no secret that they were not in it for the money, but their label – a commercial organisation after all – went with their gut feelings and allowed the band full control of shaping their records as they saw fit, happy to sit back and release what they were then given. It is perhaps one of the more equitable and impressive examples of an underground band working with a genuinely huge major record label.

First off though, it was back into a van for a drive to Los Angeles, where Warner Brothers would allow the band three weeks to compose and hone new material. Since money was now fortunately much less of an issue, MCR were lavished with plush apartments in Oakwood, LA. Around them during these recording sessions, suburban rich kids were living out vicarious fantasies at expensive, debauched parties which were "de rigueur". One might have expected Gerard Way to succumb to the vacuous charms of the Hollywood movers and shakers, essentially obnoxious child actors (whom Gerard was quoted as saying were only fifteen but drank all day), porn stars and other bands taking a break. Drugs and

> *"All the while, however, alone in his bubble Gerard was still drinking and popping pharmaceutical pills."*

alcohol were in constant supply in those suburban circles, for anyone who sought their use. Rather than follow the trend, however, Gerard and the rest of the band withdrew and stood back surveying the scene, feeling like outsiders while LA partied on in front of them. In his bubble Gerard was still often to be found having a drink however.

"Realistically, I was into being into LA when we were writing," Gerard told www.straight.com. "I knew there would be a flavour to the record as a result of living in Los Angeles for two and a half months. The phoniness and the sleaziness made a huge impact on me and the songs." What also impacted the band and Gerard in particular was being cramped in an attic, within their LA recording studio, Bay 7 in Valley Village. The attic was completely pitch black and Gerard was only armed with headphones and a microphone – an idea suggested by producer Howard Benson, in an effort to draw a soulful performance from Gerard by depriving him of outside stimuli. The technique seemed to bear fruit and credit has to go to Gerard for being open-minded enough to try it. Many rock stars would have claimed to be claustrophobic or thrown a fit and asked for some red M&Ms but not Way – he trusted the Benson method. "No one was allowed in there when I was doing my thing," Way would later tell MTV. "At first it was weird because I'm a show-off and I like people being able to watch me when I'm in the booth. But now, I can't imagine doing it any other way. I really let some intense stuff come out because I became very comfortable being naked and alone like that." On reflection, it's no surprise Way trusted Benson: the latter is a world-renowned worker of the mixing desk, having produced the likes of ska punk fiends Less Than Jake, Christian rockers POD and best of all four records with the alcohol-and-drug-fuelled rock 'n' roll behemoth known as Motörhead. His experience in analysing MCR's songs and refining certain sections and structures was vital and the band have made no secret of how much they enjoyed working with him.

One of the things the band were keen to avoid was rushing to get the record done, and Warner Brothers certainly gave them no hassle in this department. Although pleased with the debut album, MCR were happy to learn. Howard Benson thought making a record too quickly could lead an artist to feel resentful afterwards, to wish more time had been taken to try a few things in a different way. So the group were unanimous Benson had the right idea when he suggested taking a break for a few days here and there.

It was time well spent. My Chemical Romance were about to lay down a clinically righteous album, and cement their glowing reputation for some years to come.

ChAPteR 5

The Corpses Of a Thousand Evil Men

"I was like, 'I think I could run with this 'Demolition Lovers' thing.' I just felt like there needed to be this tragic, romantic, violent aspect going on in there. So I kind of married two subjects, love and revenge, and just added a slight supernatural element to that and was able to come up with basically what I think is a good metaphor for how this band operates and how we live our lives and how we feel you should live your life." Gerard Way

"The story of a man. A woman. And the corpses of a thousand evil men…" Adorned with this notorious line, My Chemical Romance's second album was introduced to the world. Released in 2004, the album was chock full of horror,

gothic rock that was perfectly glazed by Howard Benson. MCR was now a fully fledged rock act with a sound befitting their ambitions and an arsenal of songs that were exactly what the youth of the day craved. My Chemical Romance were already the band Gerard Way had dreamt of a few years previously, and they had a very specific style. Each member was easily identifiable: Ray Toro, with his afro hair so evocative of At The Drive In's Omar Rodriguez and Cedric Bixler; Mikey Way with a cute combed-forward peak à la The Count from *Sesame Street*; Matt Pelissier, with his dour sense of humour; Frank Iero, whose deep, dark eyes gave the impression he had many hidden depths. And then there was the enigmatic Gerard Way. Pasty, with reddened eyes, he was more The Crow than a glamorous new rock star – but his public wouldn't have wanted him any other way.

The singer described the music on their second album, titled *Three Cheers For Sweet Revenge*, as an explosive dose of "violent, unsafe pop music". This was certainly a most fitting description of the group themselves: they were popular and therefore pop (a point underlined by their songs' striking, catchy choruses) and they retained that edge of chaos so prevalent on the debut album. MCR's sound was still violent, resolutely unsafe and yet capable of producing beautiful sing-a-long music, with choruses that had blossomed noticeably since the first record. Where *I Brought You...* had been one huge mass of sprawling angst and, at times, interchangeable riffs and words, *Three Cheers...* was evidence of a songwriting maturity, backed up by a cast of characters who combined to unleash one of the best records of 2004. No more emo, screamo or any other form of 'mo or 'core – like many of the best acts in the musical pantheon, My Chemical Romance were simply themselves, with a sound all their own. This time, the band also had access to a budget that permitted lavish video production, and their first single, 'I'm Not Okay (I Promise)', was the best example of MCR's new-found financial backing put to good use. The song itself was a story of high-school alienation and loneliness and the video represented this perfectly with a smart take on a trailer for a movie set in a high school. Gerard spoke highly of director Marc Webb to MTV, explaining that he "came up with this idea to make a fake movie and have the video be the trailer for the fake movie. I love it. He put us in prep school. The school from *Donnie Darko* is in it. The whole thing feels like *Rushmore*. The first time we all saw it on TV, we shit ourselves." Allowing for slight exaggeration, the brothers Way and the rest of the band deserved to be proud of their foray into video making – for the striking imagery on offer ensured that anyone who hadn't yet heard or seen their performances was unlikely to stay ignorant for long – MTV, VH1, Kerrang! TV and a host of other channels religiously played the video from a song that stood out even above the other marvellous music on MCR's second LP.

"I was just swimming in this pit of despair."

Later, Gerard admitted, "It's kind of a game for us to see what we can get on the radio because if you listen to 'I'm Not Okay' it's a fucking cry for help set to a pop song." Yet because it *was* essentially a pop song, MCR got away with it and gained access to regions normally reserved for mainstream faux youth culture, where lyrics went as deep as being attracted to a girl in your school, who didn't want to know. OK, My Chemical Romance were capable of penning songs like that too, but generally in a non-sentimental manner. Everything had a sinister undertone. Way explained: "When I was writing it, I was remembering how hard it was to be a sixteen-year-old in high school... I was just swimming in this pit of despair and jealousy ... and when someone's in that situation, it's very rare that they turn to their mom or their best friend and say, 'Hey, I'm not OK. I'm in really bad shape.'" The best line of the song features a clearly frazzled Gerard, screaming the brilliant words, "I'm not o-fucking-kay!"

The theme of 'Demolition Lovers' is more fully expanded upon on *Three Cheers For Sweet Revenge*; Gerard would later confirm, "Half of it is about making a deal with the devil, the other half is taken from our experiences as a band." Those experiences were assimilated within separate chunks, often within the same songs – thus, all the songs were part of a story, though that didn't necessarily stop them working outside the album as a whole. "It really doesn't follow a linear thing," Way explained. "It's more like you're getting little snippets of the story, which at the end should make up the whole part."

Logically enough, the theme of revenge is prevalent throughout the album. Gerard has said he had been obsessed by the art of revenge ever since he heard the song by Black Flag (a group the whole of MCR admires) with that one-word title. Like most of Black Flag's material, the song's simple lyrics, coupled with the Greg Ginn guitar wall of sound, packed a mighty powerful punch – and gave them widespread appeal among punkers of all ages. "We're gonna get revenge, you won't know what hit you! Revenge! I'll watch you bleed. Revenge! That's all I'll need." Yet Henry Rollins, Greg Ginn and Black Flag were only part of Way's palette of inspiration. As he explained to *Designer*, "[On] this record particularly I looked up to Tom Waits and Nick Cave because they are very colourful, almost poetic writers, but they're also very direct. They won't use a big word if they don't have to and I like that. At the same time, though, I've been a big fan of the Pixies for years and there's a cleverness that comes with Frank Black's lyrics."

Initially the record was to be a concept album, but one event in particular changed the course of its genesis, both musically and lyrically. Gerard and Mikey's grandmother, Elena Lee Rush, passed away in November 2003 while the band were just about to begin creating *Three Cheers For Sweet Revenge*. The tragic loss changed the direction of the whole 'Demolition Lovers' theme that was originally intended to underpin the lyrics. His grandmother's passing turned Gerard's lyric writing on its head – now he decided simply to write from the heart. "In the end, listening to the record, I was like, 'Wow this record is really about loss,'" said the singer, somewhat surprised, to *Trouble Bunch*. "It took me a couple listens to really get the scope of the record and realise that it was really that blatantly about loss and death throughout almost every song. But I think death is something that we'll always write about because it's… tragic, negative and beautiful at the same time. It's very beautiful and it can be a very positive thing. It comes up very frequently on the record, to the point where people have asked me how the story ends. I'm kind of like, 'What do you think? Do you think the guy gets what he wants?'"

The song that was to open the album, and serve as an immortal reminder of the Ways' grandmother, was certainly both positive and beautiful. The boys used to call her 'Helena'; so the song was named, and eventually the track would become far bigger than the sum of its parts. "The song is about my grandmother, who passed away," Gerard told MTV, with admirable restraint, considering how many interviewers would press him for an explanation. "She was an artist, and she pushed me to be an artist. We were really close, so making the video was really good closure for me, personally. It's one of those things where I knew I was going to have to face my fears."

No easy task for such a complex man, but the woman concerned clearly warranted such a tribute. As Gerard remembered, "She was an artist and taught me pretty much everything I do today – how to sing and paint and how to perform." She bought the band their first van, because she wanted to help her two grandsons follow their dream, but when they repeatedly offered to pay her back, she wouldn't take the money. Thus the song is about celebrating the special relationship they had with her. "I knew I wanted the video to be a funeral, because I remember so much about when she died. I remember the church service being extremely upsetting. And at the cemetery, we put her in the mausoleum, and when we came outside it was sunny, like everything had changed, and I was like, 'Wow, I'm already starting to feel OK about this.'"

Gerard couldn't help feeling angry with himself, however – for missing the last year of Elena's life while he was on tour with the band. In a memorial, the Ways would manage to give their grandmother a send-off that was completely appropriate as well as being indicative of just how far My Chemical Romance had come since their early days. "We know that the video for 'Helena' is our chance to be known as a 'video' band," Gerard explained in one interview for MTV. "We could be like the Smashing Pumpkins, a band that always made these movies instead of just a bunch of guys in a basement. I think it's going to be very different from 'I'm Not Okay'. It's not funny at all. The best way to describe the video is 'very sad and celebratory, upsetting and uplifting at the same time'. It was a risk, but we've always taken risks. And this video is the biggest risk we've ever taken."

The band were determined to stick with what they knew and enlisted the services of their only director thus far, Marc Webb. In the video, MCR played pallbearers at a funeral in a rickety old church. The mourners were played by fans of the band, who applied for the part of extras through their official website, and predictably the video was swamped with black clothing, cobweb-shaped umbrellas and – naturally – thick black eyeliner. When the band launched into the chorus, the congregation rose as one, doubtless sending a shiver down the viewer's spine.

Midway through the video, a young girl rises from her coffin and performs a surreal ballerina routine. "When the girl in the coffin dances, it's really beautiful," Way told MTV. "When I watched it through the monitor I got so upset I had to leave the room. It's really sad. Because it's her last dance." The stirring scene was inspired as much by Tim Burton's gothic cinematic masterpieces as it did Guns N' Roses' famous funereal video for 'November Rain'.

Michael Rooney, the choreographer who had worked on Björk's 'It's Oh So Quiet' video was at the helm for the 'Helena' video. Gerard: "It's a funeral, so it's very sombre and very depressing, but as soon as the fast part of the song kicks in, everybody starts dancing in this Busby Berkeley style." For those unsure as to who Way was referring, Berkeley was both a movie director and a choreographer who was famous for set-pieces involving several showgirls, and also for an infamous falling out with *The Wizard Of Oz* actress Judy Garland. But the area of his work Gerard Way felt close to was Berkeley's ability to allow the audience to see parts of a routine they would not normally witness in the hands of another director. Indeed, the Los Angeles native was revered as much for the complicated geometric patterns formed by dancers that characterised his movies as his fluid camera work, which gave the viewing audience a vibrant cinematic experience rather than a staid theatrical performance.

There was another paean to the Way's grandmother within the artwork for the CD booklet. Behind the lyrics for the songs could be seen rosary beads and a cross – a mark of respect to Elena Rush, though the band still found themselves having to explain the objects' meaning and significance. As Mikey Way found out in one interview with MTV, in which he explained, "The image in the CD booklet of the rosary beads was meant as a memorial to Elena Rush, who passed away shortly before we went to Los Angeles to record the record. It's actually a scan of her rosary beads. As for my thoughts on the modern movement of Christianity, I am kind of on the fence. I'm not 100 per cent familiar with the goings on in Christianity today, as Gerard and I grew up with a Christian upbringing, and we no longer practise it. I understand the importance of faith and spirituality, but I think that each person is entitled to their own opinion… I have my own form of faith and spirituality but it isn't Christian based."

The band had written an album that they intended to be taken as a whole, and allowed the record company to choose which songs were released as singles. As Gerard would testify to *Florida Entertainment Scene*, "I think the smartest thing a band can do is not to decide what your singles are because then you don't write songs to be singles. We let the label decide. That way you can literally, honestly say to yourself we don't write singles, we write records, and you can really retain your artistic integrity that way. So we gave Warner Brothers the record literally sight unseen and said, 'Here, pick the singles, if you find any at all.'"

In many ways, *Three Cheers…* was full of potential singles, given that the momentum rarely faltered during its forty minutes and the songwriting level had improved so much since the debut album. Each track, taken on its own merit, was a standout representation of heavy rock

"I have my own form of faith and spirituality but it isn't Christian based."

music at its blackened best. As their titles would suggest, both 'You Know What They Do To Guys Like Us In Prison' and 'Thank You For The Venom' featured crushing guitar moments, short snappy solos that would be at home on a fully fledged heavy metal band's record. Lyrically, the former tackles the issue of prison rape. However there is also another side to the words, which Gerard considered were breaking boundaries by tackling the subject of crimes within prison. There is another element in evidence too – Way later suggested the idea of the song was partly influenced by a game of 'Truth Or Dare' played on the road with The Used, in which the bands' respective front men (Gerard and Bert McCracken) were obliged to kiss each other. With this in mind, the words were also references to enjoyable experiences on the road, touring with friends, and other bands who were special to MCR, such as Taking Back Sunday. Way also later revealed that it was his favourite song both on the album and to play live.

With its dedication to Elena Rose and the Christian imagery that it employs, 'Thank You For The Venom' embodied much of the flavour of the album as a whole. Though My Chemical Romance were far from being a blood-thirsty satanic heavy metal band, they saw first-hand the horror of evangelism and hardline Christianity while on tour, and the song pointed up the fact that a person deserves to make their own choice rather than being force-fed religion. Gerard's concise lyrics speak out openly in defiance of established religions, and are also a throwback to his long-held personal belief that he would lose those closest to him regardless of faith.

Elsewhere, *Three Cheers For Sweet Revenge* continued MCR's penchant for intriguing lyrical themes and sources for those themes. The song 'To The End' was inspired by a short story by William Faulkner entitled 'A Rose For Emily'. Not only was the story itself intriguing, but so too was its creator, and the song provided further evidence of Gerard's knack for drawing on a well-informed and surprising choice of stimuli. In Faulkner's story, the main character (Emily) falls in love with a man (with a notable lack of irony he is called Homer) who is presumed to be homosexual. Despite this, Emily proposes to Homer, but he declines her advances. So, as any girl would, she kills him with cyanide and sleeps with his corpse in her bedroom. Here, as with many MCR moments, there is something of the literary classics about what they do, an undercurrent of dark former times and an atmosphere of bleak and yet utterly compelling lives that fascinate the observer.

Faulkner himself was a contemporary of classic American author Ernest Hemingway, though not as well known or celebrated. Where Hemingway used a comparatively minimalist style, Faulkner's writing employed convoluted, often circuitous sentences. Although Hemingway was the better-known writer, Faulkner still won a Nobel Prize and was considered one of the twentieth century's most influential writers of fiction. His work is often referred to as obscure and challenging. Perfect for My Chemical Romance, then.

In the song 'To The End', there is a reference to an elevator that only goes up to the tenth floor. One reporter asked Gerard about this, and was told, "Well, I felt that picking a lower number would be like 'I can't get high enough', so I had to pick somewhere around ten… I felt like I just needed to get higher; like the top just isn't good enough. I think that's kind of a metaphor in how we feel and how we operate as a band, that the top isn't good enough since that's not what we're after. It's not good enough for us because we want to make a difference and actually change things. We don't just want things thrown at us."

'Hang 'Em High' was another subtle variation on the 'Demolition Lovers' theme. The female character in this song needs to know her male partner would die for her, and never lie to her. In response, he tells her if he dies he wants her to carry on and fight against the 'bad guys' the two are up against.

'I Never Told You What I Do For A Living' is one of the best tunes on the entire album, and it finishes off

proceedings perfectly. The song seems to be about a killer carefully selecting murder victims, but as with most MCR work, its trajectory is not always immediately straightforward and a range of ideas merge together over its course. The lines were typical Gerard Way, singing about loving, laughing, dancing and death; having said that, they seemed a pseudo-conceptual way of completing such a brilliant record that had been so frighteningly exciting and at the same time efficiently dispatched.

Throughout *Three Cheers For Sweet Revenge* there were tales and overtones of numerous emotions. It was a journey of love, death and destruction. There were moments of love, joy and beauty melded with death, despair, psychological issues – and the odd tale of vampirism. In other words, tailor-made for a 2004 audience who found their preferred listening matter increasingly watered down every week.

The act of creating the record alone had given My Chemical Romance a new perspective on their place in the music world. "What we really learned during this record was that whenever we experimented and tried something a little different, the songs worked really well," Way admitted afterwards. "In the future, I can see us moving even more into a rock-type realm, with lots more melody and an overall largeness. And I can see us getting even darker as far as subject matter goes."

If *I Brought You My Bullets, You Brought Me Your Love* helped to build My Chemical Romance's collective character and image in the music-loving public's eye, *Three Cheers For Sweet Revenge* revealed it as fully formed. Where could they go from here?

ChAPteR 6

A Drop of Chaos

"A lot has changed since our last tour. I got clean and sober. And it made the shows change dramatically, because my singing got a lot better... I used to drink pretty heavily in general and before shows, and that stopped. Alcohol is a depressant, so it was putting me in a really bad spot, mentally. I couldn't really tour any more if I was going to be depressed and drunk."

Gerard Way

*T*hree Cheers For Sweet Revenge was a defining statement for the world of rock music, and the public agreed with the media, who had already given MCR a healthy dose of hype to date. The record reached number 45 in the US and 34 in the UK album charts; the band took the news in good spirits but knew they had to get straight back to work and now go to promote the record in the way it deserved. My Chemical Romance appeared on radio shows the world over and played a huge sell-out tour – tastefully billed as a Taste Of Chaos. Their touring partners were The Used, Senses Fail and Underoath. In addition, they supported Green Day on the final leg of their world-touring cycle for the punk trio's *American Idiot* album.

"Oh man. Billie Joe from Green Day influenced everything about how I play guitar," Gerard Way admitted to MTV, with a laugh. "He just made it look so easy. He was the first person I aped. And if it wasn't for Green Day I wouldn't have picked up a guitar. The band couldn't believe it when we heard the news, I got the call and I was in the street in New York City and it was pouring rain, but I was just yelling and people were

"Oh man. Billie Joe from Green Day influenced everything about how I play guitar."

staring at me. And that was everybody's response. I think Bob fell down a flight of stairs when he heard the news." "It was the best of times... it was the best of times..." Mikey Way quipped on the official MCR myspace page (www.myspace.com/mychemicalromance .com) once the band had completed their tour with Green Day. By this point, Green Day had re-invented themselves completely and surpassed career album sales of more than 50 million units, so MCR really were on the road with genuine modern rock legends. As a consequence, these shows were all in cavernous arenas, rarely to less than 10,000 kids or so, and was thus a crash course on stadium rock that honed MCR's live show even further.

Ray Toro told *Concert Live Wire* that he thought, "Watching a Green Day show is really inspiring too. Like, the level of command that Billy has over the audience. The whole band. The whole audience will do whatever they want at any moment. It's incredible. And Gerard added, "I think if we had a chance to open for them doing a show in the UK with fifty, sixty thousand people, that's probably the greatest rock show ever. That would probably be the greatest to see him work sixty thousand, you know?" (In the summer of 2005, Green Day did indeed play to 65,000 people two nights in a row at Milton Keynes). And the reason Green Day asked MCR to support them? Well, it was time for a touch of mutual respect, as GD bassist Mike Dirnt explained to MTV: "We like a lot of those young punk bands, and it's flattering to hear you've influenced them, and all of them are going to forge their own path and catalogue and career history some day. But the compliments are kind of hard to take. It's like, 'Congratulations, you're old!'"

Things were about to go global for MCR, however, and in America global meant corporate sponsorship. For true corporate power you can't beat the American institution Nintendo. And so it was that one of the world's largest video game manufacturers asked My

Chemical Romance to join Lostprophets and Story Of The Year on the Nintendo Fusion Tour, beginning in the middle of September 2004. The roadshow was American consumerism in all its vast glory, showcasing Nintendo video games on huge screens in between sets by the bands. Being a part of such a momentous tour, the group members were naturally offered a host of perks. "The first day they gave us a Gamecube with four wireless controllers and *Mario Kart*, which was really nice of them, and we play that stuff all the time," said Gerard to *The Punk Site*, referring to MCR's penchant for gaming when on the road. "They just recently gave us *Donkey Konga*, the *Bongo* game, they gave us four sets of bongos so we're very excited... It definitely has its benefits."

Other benefits of the tour included, naturally, the chance to play to different types of fans, given the various genres covered by Wales' finest pop rock group act, Lostprophets, and St Louis' Story Of The Year. The former began way before MCR, in 1997, and the irony was not lost on promoters and fans alike that already My Chemical Romance were starting to overshadow several groups in supposedly similar genres, despite the fact that they were touring only their second record. SOTY had formed a year earlier than Lostprophets (though they had only changed their name from Big Blue Monkey in 2002) but were the kind of band that sometimes passed by unnoticed, especially outside America, despite their *In The Wake Of Determination* album selling 750,000 copies by December 2005. My Chemical Romance managed to top that figure, however. By the end of their touring cycle, they had shifted 800,000 sales units for *Three Cheers For Sweet Revenge*, and the figure was on the rise constantly.

✳ ✳ ✳ ✳ ✳

Behind the scenes, the touring lifestyle was beginning to take its toll. "Things started to spiral out of control," Gerard admitted to www.straight.com later. "It started to get the best of me. So the same way I was functioning just to sing when we were doing the record, I functioned just to play the shows when we did Warped. By the end of tour, what I was doing to myself was affecting my performances, my appearance, and my energy... the shows were amazingly great, but there were definitely a few that I don't even remember playing."

The pressures reached their greatest when Gerard attended a show by The Killers. According to an interview with Gerard himself in *Alternative Press*, the singer took cocaine before the concert then found himself in the middle of the street vomiting everywhere. "My head was pounding, it felt twice its size," Way recalled, "all the veins in my head felt like they were going to explode. The next day I woke up and I was more suicidal than I had ever been in my entire life, and it was amazing to me." Such a tale being printed in a high profile magazine was a shock for his fans in many ways, even though he had never pretended to be something he wasn't. His openness has to be applauded. Gerard assumed nobody in the band really knew, but they must have had an idea, especially his kid brother Mikey who later commented, "I think I was accepting it because I was as bad as he was at one point. I was even worse than him at some points early on in the band's career. I thought it would be really hypocritical to say, 'Put the vodka down!'" Frank Iero was understanding too, saying "Any time you mix drinking with narcotics, something bad can happen," he told *Alternative Press*. "And depression, mixing the three of them is really bad. Every time you do it, it changes your whole body chemistry."

Manager Brian Schechter managed to talk Way out of his mire. Shortly before leaving for a tour of Japan, a place Gerard had always wanted to visit, the vocalist admitted he was "terrified. All I did for two days was drank, swallowed pills and loaded up for the trip." 'Loading up' according to that article in *Alternative Press*, included drinking at the airport bar then ingesting a whole bar of Xanax; Way eventually fell asleep before waking up in a completely different country. Xanax is generally used to treat anxiety and depression and, like most treatments for the ailment, makes the user drowsy and lethargic. Gerard somehow ghosted through customs, before performing two gigs in the country very much worse for wear – yet all press reports still review these shows (remarkably) as awesome. MCR seem to have the ability to pull amazing live shows out of the bag regardless of extenuating circumstances and this is a key reason why they have become one of the biggest new rock bands on the planet. Frank Iero later revealed to *Alternative Press*, "It was weird, because usually when we're playing me and Gerard can look at each other and no matter what's going on I can pull back to it and go for it. When I looked for him in Osaka and he was underneath the stage there ... I just wanted to put my guitar down and go."

"I walked offstage and I threw up straight for 45 minutes into this garbage can, like I had never thrown up before."

The unpleasant side-effects of over-indulgence were yet to fully manifest themselves however, as Gerard told *Alternative Press*: "I walked offstage and I threw up straight for 45 minutes into this garbage can, like I had never thrown up before. I puked everything out." The management were concerned and swiftly started to talk about calling a doctor – MCR's manager Brian Schechter is rightly now seen as one of modern music's most astute and accomplished businessmen and managers. Meanwhile, sitting in his own sick and feeling very down and exhausted, Gerard realised that enough was enough. He later cited that moment as a key turning point.

While many would simply scream "Rock 'n' roll!" – after all, isn't this just the kind of thing that rock stars 'do'? – it didn't take a genius to figure out that Way would be suffering very soon if he continued with this lifestyle. A host of talented young rock stars have died from excess. They might garner admiration for their music, their lyrics and even their personalities, but it would be a strange fellow who felt Kurt Cobain was a god for being a heroin addict who shot himself, that Jimi Hendrix was a hero for choking on his own vomit, or that Jim Morrison deserved praise for gorging himself to death with a lethal concoction of drugs and alcohol. None of the aforementioned lived to see thirty.

Jimi Hendrix, in true higher-than-mighty-rock-star fashion, once wrote the lyric, "I'm the one that has to die when it's time for me to die, so let me live my life, the way I want to." This was a theme every one of the musicians above would identify with, and to some extent so would many musicians who didn't feel the need to use drink or drugs to enjoy themselves. But self-destruction is undeniably rife among rock stars who find themselves too famous too early and cannot handle the pressure, the touring, or who simply lose the plot. Impressively, Gerard Way did not intend to join that list, however incredible the company was. "I didn't know what was going to happen when I got back to the US," he admitted to *Alternative Press*. "I got off the plane and was really upset ... At the same time I didn't know if I was going to be *alive* the next day. I said goodbye to everybody and I had tears in my eyes because I wasn't really sure if I was going to see anybody in my band again." Aside from this, MCR were about to part ways with a founder member and this return flight from Japan would prove to be another pivotal moment (more of which below).

"(Gerard) made the active decision. He picked up the phone and called me at one of his darkest moments and said, 'This has got to stop,'" Brian Schechter says of Gerard's decision to quit drinking. "And he has remained very certain and very true to it." It was the MCR manager, alongside Gerard's band mates, who helped the singer tackle his issues and soon he was commanding stages everywhere again – this time completely straight. "He's the guy who got me clean and sober," Way told *Alternative Press*. "It was a really big risk; I don't think they knew how bad I was." The singer also admitted that he had become somewhat defensive about his lifestyle. "I knew it was the only way I'd stay alive. I felt like I'd created something that people expected and it gets overwhelming. I felt like I'd taken away my only safety net. The best thing right now is I'm really clear headed." Going on to a public platform stone-cold sober must have been a surreal reality check, but not only did Gerard Way see sense at a young age, his sobriety made My Chemical Romance a better unit. Further, his ability to sort himself out and his manager's and fellow band members' belief in him, reinforced MCR's legendary 'cool gang' reputation. Everyone from the band to their fans soon realised the intensity and passion of a live show had *not* been improved by Gerard's lifestyle: the same high-octane performance level was there. MCR was all about playing their guts out.

The band still had to make an important decision regarding another of their number, however – the drummer. The rest of MCR have never confirmed exactly why Matt Pelissier and they parted ways. Ray Toro: "It was like the moment you break up with someone you've been dating for three or four years that you used to love in the beginning of the relationship and things went sour but for some reason you are still together." It was Toro, along with Brian Schechter who travelled to Pelissier's house. The drummer later revealed to *Alternative Press* that the last time he had seen – or even heard from – Gerard was with their hug at the airport on returning from Japan. Comments and interviews in the press since the split have voiced different reasons for why this founder member parted ways from MCR. Moreover, for many bands, such a change in personnel at a time when things were going so well could have proved terminal. Fortunately, it didn't.

Toro said of the lack of an official announcement ahead of the news breaking that "People probably thought it was weird that we didn't make any kind of statement beforehand or really talk about what happened. It must have been weird for people to notice 'Wow! One of the people who started the band and has been in it for three years has gone and they didn't say anything.'" He went on to say they had not wanted to trade discussions over the matter in the press.

Pelissier's replacement was one Bob Bryar. Born December 31, 1979, in Chicago, Illinois, Bryar is the only MCR member to come from outside New Jersey.

The band met him during an early tour with The Used, when he was working as a drum tech. The arrival of a new drummer just fired the band up even more – as if they needed it.

* * * * *

In November 2005, My Chemical Romance decided to play a free show (sponsored by Los Angeles radio giant KROQ-FM) in the parking lot of the city of Orange, California (official motto: "A Slice of Old Town Charm"). Although it was a welcome event for several thousand Californian fans, the gig did nothing to endear the authorities to MCR. "The Orange police said that we were trying to incite a riot and that we used excessive foul language, and they threatened to arrest us for trespassing," Gerard said afterwards. "They were giving us a hard time all day. And after we finished playing, the police said that we would never be allowed to play in the city of Orange again." Perhaps predictably, The Orange Police Department had a very different account of what had transpired. OPD Sergeant Dave Hill: "The supervising officer who was over there told me that My Chemical Romance began their show with a profanity-laced tirade. Not just profanity, but vulgarity. I guess I just draw a distinction between an arena show, where you pay money to get in and hear them curse at you, and an open-air concert in the parking lot of Best Buy, where grandmas and grandpas are walking by and saying, 'Oh my gosh, listen to what's coming out of their mouths.'"

Best Buy, a slightly more hi-tech version of Walmart, was perhaps not the most appropriate store outside which to scream "I'm not o-fucking-kay", but MCR was there to play for people who understood their act. This was not just a gig – there was to be a planned signing session afterwards. The plans soon went awry, however: there were too many people to please, and those in charge of security suggested the session should be truncated as there could be a 'security issue' if it were left unattended. Gerard Way and My Chemical Romance didn't see things the same way, though. Way promised that "Even if it took all night to meet everybody, we would do it. You don't want to promise people anything and then turn your back on that promise. So when I got onstage, I told everyone that we were going to play, dry off and then meet up with everybody."

Brian Schechter was visibly pleased by the turnout and couldn't help admiring his band's commitment to please each and every one of their growing fan base. He remarked to *Pollstar*, "Every time they play, there's more and more kids singing along, and they meet more and more kids that say, 'Your band's helped me through some of the hardest, darkest times of my life.' That's why they started the band – to help kids the way that music helped them when they were having tough times. Sometimes they get inundated with press requests and radio requests and meet-and-greets and promos. They get a little frazzled by it, but they never complain."

From Florida to Alaska the same media questions kept on attempting to destroy any remaining brain cells

My Chemical Romance: Something Incredible This Way Comes

Undeniably the central focus of the band, Gerard Way – for the first two
albums he was dressed as an archetypal black-haired rocker.

Constant touring and incendiary live shows have
established MCR's reputation around the globe

The band's relationship with their fans is the stuff of music biz legend...

... although the presents they receive can be a little odd.

Ballerinas and roses, all part of the theatrical MCR stage show for the *Three Cheers For Sweet Revenge* album tour.

Gerard Way: arguably *the* most enigmatic and photogenic
frontman of recent years

Critical acclaim for their third album *The Black Parade* means that MCR
will triumph at dozens of award shows ... no longer the outsiders?

My Chemical Romance: the biggest band on the planet?

My Chemical Romance still possessed after the mind-numbingly long tours, with banal observations such as the fact that some people may perceive MCR to be a 'self-destructive band', an idea inspired by the onstage violence that is frequently a part of their gigs. Frank Iero rebutted those claims forcefully in one interview for www.radiotakeover.com: "I have an answer for that. There is a Norwegian black metal band called Mayhem. The singer of this band takes shards of glass and cuts himself up, whatever. That is self-abuse and self-destruction. And that is the message that I'm sure that he wants to send to people, that hurting yourself is cool. Getting pleasure from pain. There are tons of bands that probably get pleasure from pain. When we get hurt we want people to know it's accidental. If you lose yourself and go off, sometimes people get hurt and it's just a risk you take. If you go nuts, odds are you get hurt."

It wasn't just that one band in Norway who were visual psychopaths onstage, either. In fact, black metal was notorious for being a genre emphatically not for the weak and faint-hearted. A case in point: Kristian Vikernes (later named Varg Vikernes, and also Count Grishnackh) was once a member of Mayhem, but subsequently went on to form his own band, Burzum. Musically the group certainly appealed to black-metal enthusiasts, but Vikernes was eventually to become far more renowned as… a murderer. He killed former friend and Mayhem member Øystein Aarseth (also known as Euronymous), allegedly with 23 stab wounds – two to the head, five to the neck, and sixteen to the back.

He was also imprisoned for taking part in arson attacks on several churches (a catalyst that helped the whole Norwegian black metal scene to erupt in the first place) and sentenced to 21 years – the maximum sentence passable under Norwegian law – in Trondheim Fengsel prison, Norway.

Other bands under the black-metal flag included everyone from Dissection (who could also be classified as death metal) to Emperor. The former featured Jon Nödtveidt on vocals and guitar. In 1998, Nödtveidt was convicted of murder and sentenced to prison for six years. Emperor featured one Bard Faust in its ranks (as well as Samoth, who was active in a spate of church-burning in Norway in the early Nineties), who was to become notorious for stabbing a homosexual man to death.

"Clearly My Chemical Romance were utterly tame in comparison to such extreme bands."

Clearly My Chemical Romance were utterly tame in comparison to such extreme bands. Hurting themselves onstage, if and when it was deliberate, was merely a cathartic outlet in line with playing the music itself. It was no different to a 'cutter', someone who sees slicing themselves with a razor blade and witnessing their own blood dripping down their flesh as a way of letting tension out, or – more extremely – trepanning, the art of drilling a hole in the head to release pressure.

A rock band, who were commercial enough to be 'allowed' to swamp MTV and numerous mainstream magazines – however dangerous – was never going to compete with genuinely scary black metallers, just as they couldn't outdo the kind of person who fancied walking around with part of their head missing. As Gerard patiently explained to www.radiotakeover.com, "There was a time where I used to cut myself and that, but I've gotten over it. I mean, people who do that have a problem and it's not the right way to deal with it. It's sometimes the easy way out, but it doesn't mean it's the right way."

It was no different to someone who sees slicing themselves with a razor blade and witnessing their own blood dripping down their flesh as a way of letting tension out.

Gerard also referred to the fact that when the band started, the need to work out stress through pain onstage was paramount, but that My Chemical Romance had since become a lot smarter and even selective about their choice of performance. Further, he openly admitted that when they had first started, he was going through a lot of pain *every* night on stage.

And therein lay the secret of MCR's mass appeal to hundreds of thousands of comparative strangers, spread over a wide range of ages. Instead of cutting oneself and screaming blue murder for the sake of it, there was a cleaner, healthier and downright more enjoyable way of kicking against the pricks: go out there and show off your talent. As Frank Iero would muse to www.radiotakeover.com, "So many kids have come up and told us that there are things in their [lives] that have been destroyed and from our thirty-five minute set they have figured some things out. If we can do that to one kid a night, we're done." In the grand scheme of things, a short set by a rock 'n' roll band was nothing much, but it was all about what they did in that time span. My Chemical Romance knew no limits in their quest to get their message across – but, Gerard asserted, "It's fucking worth the trip, it's fucking worth two thousand dollars of broken equipment, a fucking busted nose, everything. All of that."

One notable, if slightly bizarre, incident of 2005 occurred when Gerard was set upon by a blackbird at a hotel called The Phoenix in San Francisco before a show. "Craziest thing that ever happened to me was being attacked by that black bird," he told www.metalunderground.com. "It pecked the shit out of my head. We were leaving to go to a show the next morning and the bird just fuckin' attacked my head. And the next day Slipknot were there, they were coming in as we were leaving, and they got attacked by birds too…"

Now *that's* the kind of violence My Chemical Romance can do without…

ChAPteR 7

The New Breed

"You see us playing these songs about fictitious gunfights, cowboys, electric chairs, about getting fucked in jail. The abstraction is there for a reason. It's for people to get what they want out of it. This band is therapy for us. What we're saying through the performance is, 'This can or cannot be therapy for you, too. Either way, we'll still do it.'" Gerard Way

In 2004, Gil Kaufman wrote an article on www.mtv.com in which he suggested there was a new wave of 'boy bands' sweeping the musical world. Except that this type of boy group was not the archetypal version – say, The Backstreet Boys or an older era of boy band such as New Kids On The Block.

Instead, thanks partly to MTV, the so-called punk-pop bands of the modern era were taking over from those acts who were once known for being a band of four or five members, who lip-synched and danced their way into girls' (and boys') hearts around the world, selling millions of records in the process and making bland, saccharine, radio-friendly pop music only a housewife or adolescent could love.

So we now no longer had Jordan Knight, the Adonis-like lead singer of one of the first boy bands, New Kids On The Block – it was now over to the likes of Benji and Joel Madden of Good Charlotte – all tattoos, piercings and 'alternative' clothing. Backstreet Boys, along with Boyz II Men, are the only boy bands to have sold over 50 million records – a milestone few, if any, of the modern pop-punk phenomenon are likely to reach. But the essential argument by Kaufman was sound. In the modern era, it was not so much about "hot dance moves and matching threads" and more about originality and realness. Kaufman included My Chemical Romance as a "new boy band" along with Good Charlotte, Sum 41, Simple Plan and Dashboard Confessional.

"It's definitely weird," observed Gerard Way to the same site, "I guess we are taking the place of the boy bands and pin-ups, so these girls now have these dysfunctional heroes on their wall. We always thought we'd be underground or on the fringes, so we're shocked by it." Perhaps it is instinct for an artist such as Gerard to expect to be an underground phenomenon at best. How often had heavy music truly been in the mainstream

radar, aside from very rare and spectacular success stories such as Metallica or Def Leppard? And even then, some felt that those bands were more commercial (especially Leppard) than MCR and as such, were intrinsically far more likely to hit the big time. Metallica only truly broke through into mainstream popularity with their self-titled fifth album, which eschewed their speed-metal roots. But with the sheer choice of multi-genre music channels on offer in the developed world, the boundaries between underground and mainstream were becoming increasingly hazy, and My Chemical Romance was just the sort of band to be able to appeal to both sets of listeners. A viewer with a cable remote control could flick across an array of music channels and be hit with anything from the latest hip-hop cut to the in-your-face style of My Chemical Romance; it was clear that music was undergoing a new era of open-mindedness. When MTV acknowledge you are crossing boundaries, it means you have done a damn fine job so far, given that a corporate music video channel can assist or kill a band's career.

Of course, it was not just the visual representation of a band that was important. Radio had become, for a time at least, somewhat less important for heavy rock bands, for one reason in particular: real heavy rockers were never played on regular, commercial radio stations. You only have to look at MCR's heroes Iron Maiden for an example of how radio treated a heavy metal institution. From their early days of trying to be heard, right through to actually being one of the biggest heavy metal bands of all time, they were almost *never* played on a commercial radio station. The same was also true of lesser lights such as Status Quo and other rock 'dinosaurs'. So it's clear there had been a real shift in the attitudes of those controlling the playlists.

Gil Kaufman had given the 'new' boy bands credit for invading the video channels, and the same was also true of radio. Initially a band, however raucous, would find their first songs played on college radio – as was the case with My Chemical Romance and 'Vampires (Will Never Hurt You).' That's often where they would stay until, suddenly, the radio stations made a critical decision that was as baffling as it was refreshing. They too began to select bands based on their image, on whether they were cool or uncool. Listening tastes were being dictated by radio stations despite the fact that you can't see a band's image on the radio! But whereas this attitude harmed the likes of Iron Maiden (who still sold huge numbers, regardless of radio play), it was a godsend for groups such as My Chemical Romance, who benefited from radio exposure worldwide.

Moreover, the radio was equally a blessing for anyone who enjoyed listening to new music that way and, more so than any other platform, it was radio that blurred supposedly clear genres. When you heard a song, especially if you didn't know who it was by, you either liked it or you didn't. Taste was the defining factor in whether a song was good or not, and not how it was dressed up. Ultimately the general music fan who was not so concerned with being a real 'punk' per se could immerse himself in a Green Day song and be part of that lifestyle, even for only a three-minute period. Gerard Way seemed ambivalent about the question of whether MCR was a punk band or not, claiming with some degree of authority and sensibility, to *Concert Live Wire*, that it was "how you live your life, how you choose to live your life, decisions that you make. *If* you even decide to acknowledge it as punk rock instead of acknowledging it as just being yourself. That's all it means to us because it's become such a marketing thing now... It's a good thing because it makes people aware of it. It's a bad thing because people make money off of it and it's not kind of what it's founded on. Shit. I mean, an old lady in the suburbs who decides to stop mowing her lawn because the town tells her to 'cause she likes the long grass... that's punk rock."

So, the ultimate question for all underground aficionados was: were bands such as My Chemical Romance selling out by posing for *Alternative Press* (which has always been a key supporter of underground music, often against all mainstream trends) or *Kerrang!*, or making videos to be shown on primetime music channels? Should a supposedly underground band even *make* a music video? Some – the minority – would say no; others would say no too, unless the video was particularly worthy; the majority would probably concur that videos were for the most part entertaining and made no difference to how good a band actually was.

Gerard Way eloquently explained the MCR take on selling your soul for the corporate dollar to *Concert Live Wire*: "Selling out is selling out your beliefs for something. It's not standing up for yourself. It's letting people shape and manipulate you into what they want so they can use you and make money. Writing a song to write a single is selling out. Writing a record because it's what you feel, isn't. We tend to get this question a lot now because that's the general perception of selling out. It's just like all of a sudden you get big or popular, you sold out. I mean, I don't think Green Day sold out and they're the biggest band on the planet and they started as a band playing in basements just like us.

"As a side note," he continued, "[there are] also indie labels that treat bands worse than majors and it's kind of an unsaid thing in the community because you see commercials on TV by labels saying they're fighting high corporate rock and they've treated their bands worse than corporate rock. I think people really need to become more aware of what's really going on instead of what they tell you on commercials 'cause I think that's how actually a lot of people are getting educated by propaganda, you know?"

"We're a band that wants to reach a shit load of people."

The band's attitude to signing with Warners is in itself punk rock. By not actually giving a damn about what myopic 'indie' purists were saying, MCR sent out a message loud and clear. They unswervingly made it clear that they wanted to get their music out to as many people as possible and still vehemently maintained creative control over the most minute of details. This, in the modern rock world, is how it should be done.

Gerard had a point. My Chemical Romance were one of the few bands who had managed to embrace their underground nature, and maintain a gargantuan fan base, as well as making appearances on most major pop video channels. It helped that they were a relatively new group, and so had not had years to build a reputation of being a certain type of band (unlike Metallica, who were vilified for changing their staple sound of ten years so radically). Ultimately, however, it was down to the attitude and the music itself. My Chemical Romance excelled on all levels. "A label like Warner Brothers, especially in the underground community is looked at as this mammoth machine that chews up and spits people out," Gerard observed to *Crush Music* magazine. "Warner Brothers is extremely proud of us because they're excited to have a real band again."

The post-Millennial music market saw a sea-change of attitudes towards bands such as MCR. Gone were the days when mainstream artists won all the marketing budgets and spends ahead of their more alternative label-mates; now, the accountants who ran most major record labels realised that the alternative niche was actually a seam of passion that equated to billions of dollars of sales every year. Thus, a band like MCR can find themselves sitting on the same group of record labels as Madonna; an act like green Day can find themselves the biggest selling rock band on the planet; and tours such as Vans Warped continually prove capable of pulling in hundreds of thousands of fans.

"Warners is such a family and such a team effort," Gerard mused. "We deal with a very small group of people. I'm sure there's other A&Rs and other people at that label that work other acts that are very commercial. Acts like Ashlee Simpson, I don't think she's on Warner Brothers but you know what I mean. [Ironically, Ashlee Simpson later told Mikey Way that she had the *Three Cheers...* album.] The people that we work with wanted to work something very real."

Perhaps in MCR's case, and indeed in the case of many other bands who have emerged from nowhere to make their stamp on rock, the real problem in suddenly being touted as a 'sell out' was the distancing that this usually meant from the humble fanzine. Nowhere is the cut-and-paste 'zine more prevalent, or more important, than in the punk rock community. A 'zine is an achievable goal for virtually anybody with a computer, some money for printing and a vision of where they want it to go. When bands are first starting off they often do interviews with as many 'zines as possible because, let's face it, most bands only ever stay rooted in the underground so they need as much publicity as possible – from the bottom up. The real uproar seems to arise when a band is plucked from fanzine world into the glossy, newsstand magazine arena. Despite the fact there are some very fine full-colour glossies out there covering rock music, it's an understandable point. But then again, why be in a band if you don't want to be successful? My Chemical Romance seem to have the right attitude when it comes to dealing with all of the scene politics inevitably thrown their way. Yes, they were a band with a punk attitude, but they were also quite willing to represent a major label if it meant being heard by more people. And that's certainly what had happened since they became attached to Warner Brothers.

Besides, Warners (who, ironically, own the Cartoon Network) had a good reputation as far as representing bands goes. Not only did they preside over the likes of the Red Hot Chili Peppers in their most productive phase – which produced the stone-cold classic *Blood Sugar Sex Magik* (and, later *By The Way*) – they also found themselves embroiled in a legal case over Ice T's metal outfit, Bodycount. In the UK at the time of writing, Warner Records UK's Managing Director is Korda Marshall, a man heavily involved in the discovery and signing of such pioneering acts as Muse, Garbage, Pop Will Eat Itself and Ash. Famed for keeping his nose to the ground despite being one of UK music's most powerful faces, Marshall is a personalised example of why Warners' corporate ethics work.

Warner Brothers is not just about Bugs Bunny cartoons and modern big-budget Hollywood movies such as *Troy* and the remake of *The Phantom Of The Opera*. It also owns the Time Warner subsidiary, which in turn, owned everything from AOL to CNN. Warners' annual revenue in 2005 was listed at a staggering $42.1 billion. Yet their attitude to artists seems sound: MCR were still allowed to do their own thing, unhampered by the corporate hand.

* * * * *

That nagging 'emo' reference – now completely inappropriate for the type of music MCR played – still surfaced in tandem with the band's name from time to time. It was usually by huge and necessarily corporate companies such as www.launch.com, but Gerard wasn't too perplexed by their faux pas, patiently telling *The Punk Site*, "I mean, Launch.com is owned by Yahoo!, which is this really huge corporation thing. I'm sure that they have a hard time categorising music and they're probably just going off what they find in the media to call bands like ours, you know? The main reason we get categorised in that [way] is 'cause we tour with so many of those bands." Whatever bill you see MCR performing on, it is hard to maintain that they are still 'emo'. They have now successfully ploughed their own furrow and are beginning to gestate – like all great bands – their own sound. They don't sound emo, they don't sound metal, they just sound like My Chemical Romance. The continuation of this uniqueness will be critical if the band are to continue evolving at such a rate. Such indivduality will also guarantee them longevity long after any emo phase or similar has been and gone. My Chemical Romance are assuredly no fad. Despite only having two albums to their name, they are seemingly here to stay and their success so far has made them all the more determined to underline their lyrics with issues that matter, as they have done from day one.

Needless to say, the gothic attire sported by many in MCR's audiences borrowed heavily from the kind of world-view that Tim Burton dreamt up for his movies. There have been some photo shoots of Gerard Way that show him with a blood-spattered face and heavy make-up – at times looking like the perfect Edward Scissorhands. Edward's creator, Tim Burton, is arguably the cinematic equivalent of My Chemical Romance. His designs – in everything from *The Nightmare Before Christmas* (1993) to 2005's *Corpse Bride* – were striking and instantly recognisable as a Burton creation, but also there were many other aspects of his imagery that seemed to go hand in hand with MCR. The script of *Corpse Bride* features a host of lines that could easily have come from the pen of Gerard Way – for example, "Die, die, we all pass away, But don't wear a frown, Because it's really okay, You might try and hide, And you might try to pray, But we all end up the remains of the day." On the surface of it, Burton's animated works (as opposed to the big-budget movies he had also presided over, such as *Batman*) were aimed at children, but there

"Anything shoved in your face as a teen, you're going to rebel against."

was a distinctly dark undercurrent, an uneasiness, that permeated almost every area of his work. Quite simply, Burton sided with the 'freaks' and all those from high school and beyond who had also been castigated with that generic, overused term, felt empathy with the cinematic scenarios he created. Perhaps the most strikingly similar offering to the work of My Chemical Romance was Burton's book *The Melancholy Death of Oyster Boy & Other Stories*, which featured tales about misfit children with names such as Oyster Boy, Match Girl and Stainboy. Coincidently, but ironically, in the book Stainboy is said to have once had his own flash cartoon series on www.atomfilms.com (an anorak's movie website).

Needless to say, MCR's look has influenced their fans' fashion sense too. As Anne Ichikawa, entertainment editor for *Elle Girl* magazine, explained, "When I was growing up, we all loved Eddie Vedder and Kurt Cobain, and then Britney Spears and Backstreet Boys happened and I think it's back to a backlash against that now. Anything shoved in your face as a teen, you're going to rebel against. It's cool for girls not to be mainstream now, it's cool to dress a certain way and look for something different. The idea is the same – some guy in a band to fixate on — but they just look different now." This may be true, but it's also part of the familiar tale of rebellion stretching back throughout history: kids always find ways to deliberately piss their parents off, or rebel against regular 'straight' society. It just seemed that, come 2005, it was more acceptable to be pierced, tattooed or goth-ed up to the eyeballs while doing so. Not that Gerard Way was likely to bring sharp objects anywhere near his skin: he is terrified of needles. He was even quoted as saying that "nipple rings freak me out". Frank Iero, on the other hand, has many tattoos and piercings, including a tattoo of the letters "N" and "J" inside his lip (representing New Jersey), a jack-o-lantern, which he got on his 18th birthday, and the word 'Halloween' tattooed across his fingers (one finger has two 'L's so that the word fits neatly). It's perhaps no coincidence that Iero was born on Halloween or that his pumpkin-shaped tattoo brings to mind Tim Burton's *The Nightmare Before Christmas* creation, the smiling jack-o-lantern protagonist Jack Skellington.

Some time after *Three Cheers For Sweet Revenge*, My Chemical Romance took to wearing uniforms onstage, looking like a darker version of Swedish garage rockers The Hives (who wear black-and-white suits). The reason was not simply for a more clear-cut image – rather, it was an idea that grew with time, along with the band. The catalyst sprung from Gerard beating his personal problems. Frank had told one interviewer, "when Gerard got clean and sober and when we got Bob in the band it was almost important for us to be in the same gang. We needed it. We needed it for ourselves." Guitarist Ray Toro was in agreement and told *Concert Live Wire*, "When all that went down there was definitely a sense of unity among all of us that was never there before and I think it was just good to have a visual representation that staged the show with solidarity like a focus we all had and shared together."

MCR might well be part of a movement for which gothic chic is now acceptable, but they have just as much in common with certain rock bands of the late Eighties, specifically Axl Rose and his band Guns N' Roses. A crazy comparison? Well, consider: there has been no new Guns N' Roses material proper since 1993's *The Spaghetti Incident?* covers album. The public is crying out for bands who have something insightful to say and who rock harder than a ten-ton hammer. In both Gerard and Axl you have a compelling artist – you never quite know what either of them is going to come up with next. Fans can identify with both Rose and Way as artists who have experienced many similar hardships to themselves and have come out the other side, better for their tribulations. As Guns N' Roses' original guitarist Slash once said, "Anything we have to go through is worth it to get a good song out of it." In fact, Gerard has become something of a demi-god to his fans. With all due respect to the other members of the band, MCR would probably survive if any of the members except the lead singer departed – another obvious similarity to Axl Rose who, as fate would have it, is the only original remaining member of Guns N' Roses at the time of writing.

✳ ✳ ✳ ✳ ✳

For a good idea of MCR's crossover appeal, go to www.myspace.com, where anyone in the world can sign up (as themselves or anyone they want to pretend to be) and create a page all their own, all under the 'myspace' banner. The site has become a global trend with millions of users. Each user has a number of friends on their page, and the pages are neatly split between personal and commercial users. There is a music section in which almost every band in the world that is active (plus many others who have now split up) seems to have a page. MCR are no slouches and boasted an impressive 435,000 fans as of February 2006 and an unprecedented 4,268,376 hits on their page. The only problem is, whereas the www.myspace.com/mychemicalromance page is the official myspace, people inevitably pretend to be members of the band and confuse an awful lot of fans. Mikey Way had to make a statement on the official page in a 'blog', in which he stated that: "I, Michael Way, have never, and will never have an account on myspace.com." Apparently some people have been creating myspace profiles under the guise of various members of My Chemical Romance. "Unless I've been sleepwalking, these are absolutely positively NOT ME" he said.

It's just one more example of the kind of over-the-top devotion this band can inspire. Ultimately, of course, MCR were there for their fans and they certainly did not consider themselves any better than their followers. Gerard summed it up perfectly when he was quoted on www.punknews.org: "If for one minute you think you're better than a sixteen-year-old girl in a Green Day T-shirt, you are sorely mistaken. Remember the first time you went to a show and saw your favourite band. You wore their shirt, and sang every word. You didn't know anything about scene politics, haircuts, or what was cool. All you knew was that this music made you feel different from anyone you shared a locker with. Someone finally understood you. This is what music is about."

ChAPteR 8

Death
Warmed Up

*"Our message is simple, and one that we always
portray: keep yourself alive and always have hope.
If people see through the doom and gloom they will
find the light at the end of the tunnel. The idea
behind* Three Cheers For Sweet Revenge *was to
tell a fictional story that mirrored the first two years
of our lives. To execute the message we use metaphors,
such as the supernatural element of resurrection.
People should be allowed to think for themselves...
We like to give our fans more credit than most people
would and let them figure out what's right and
wrong on their own."* Gerard Way

On December 26, 2004, a massive tsunami hit
Indonesia, Thailand, Malaysia and further
beyond. Brought about by an oceanic
earthquake, the disaster was the deadliest in history
claiming the lives of a massive approximated 275,000

people. My Chemical Romance wanted to make a contribution to the charity (Music For Relief) set up by nu-metal stars Linkin Park to benefit victims and families of the tsunami. So it was that in early 2005, MCR surprised their fans by recording a cover version of the 1981 Queen & David Bowie classic 'Under Pressure' with The Used.

"It was Bert McCracken's idea," Gerard revealed. "A few months ago he had mentioned covering 'Under Pressure' and I was like, 'That's a cool idea. I love Queen, I love Bowie so the best of both worlds, it's a duet. Sounds great, let's do it.' Then the tsunami happened and we realised there was actually a purpose for this song, we can use it to raise money for the tsunami so then it became more about that. That was really awesome that we were able to help out with this song." [The track was available on www.apple.com/itunes, the digital download facility where people pay for albums or individual tracks, all for use on the Apple i-Pod, and every time a download was ordered, a donation was also made to Music for Relief.] In fact, iTunes was the only place you could purchase the song – rather than promoting the band, this was all about the charity contributions. Quite simply, to download the song you paid a small fee and the money all helped Music For Relief raise as much as possible.

Needless to say, the song was completely different to the usual MCR fare, but they managed to make it their own, with a slightly quicker tempo, some well-placed sound effects and a glorious crescendo towards the end of the track when Gerard utters the lines, "Can't we give

ourselves one more chance? Why can't we give love that one more chance?" Amazingly, the song has now spanned three generations: those who were alive and remembered the original song; anyone unfortunate enough to have heard Vanilla Ice take the main tune from the song for his 'Ice Ice Baby' hit single; and now, a newer generation who heard the superb take on the original by Way, McCracken and Co. This was a version Queen's late vocalist Freddy Mercury would surely have endorsed.

"Two bands in two separate countries, we had a very small window of opportunity in which to do it. Two of my guys flew out a day early to LA before we started some tour and I was out there and did my vocals," Gerard explained to *NME*. "The Used based off of our template of the song, put their parts over it and then it was together. We didn't play it live together until a week into the Taste of Chaos tour. It was pretty much let's go ahead and do this. We tried it for two soundchecks then we played it live." McCracken also suggested to Gerard that the two join together live to play the song and forge even greater awareness. He didn't mean MCR either – it was simply going to be Gerard and The Used. "I was extremely nervous 'cause I've never played with anybody besides my band, I've never really been in other bands,"

"For people to go and put it on the internet and have people download it is a bit of a bummer."

Gerard admitted. "We just pulled it off. We practiced two separate days during sound check and I was still really nervous and then Brandon from The Used, the drummer was the one that believed in it the most and he was like, 'No, we can do this,' and then we went out and did it and it was amazing. I think it's super cool 'cause you don't see that kind of thing any more. You see a lot of competitiveness, you see a lot of bands talking shit about other bands, you don't see bands come together for one purpose very often, especially in a live sense."

And the MCR front man thought it would benefit the crowds watching the song live, as much as it would help charitable causes: "I think people walk away from that less aggressive and go, 'That was really cool. I didn't know all the words to it. I didn't mosh to it but it was a really beautiful song and when am I ever going to see these two bands on the same stage again.'"

MCR would soon spread their name and good reputation even further with two music videos, for 'The Ghost Of You' and 'You Know What They Do To Guys Like Us In Prison'. Unfortunately however, before it was quite ready for release it became available on the internet – such was the anticipation for My Chemical Romance's next visual epic. "It's not such a bad problem to have people wanting to see our video so badly that they're trying to find it on the internet or leak it," Gerard Way said, in good humour, to MTV. "Sure you're bummed artistically, because it's not finished, but it's a pretty awesome problem. There's so much buzz about it that people can't wait." Frank Iero wasn't so easy-going about the video being sent across airwaves worldwide when it was not the finished, fully glossed product: "It's like painting a picture, and you're not done with it yet, but someone shows it in an art exhibition. It's the art that you make, and if you don't feel that it's done, for people to go and put it on the internet and have people download it is a bit of a bummer. It was pretty much finished, but there were still little finishing touches that if you saw it now, you wouldn't even notice they were there, but I noticed them."

The band most definitely did have full creative control on their official website, www.mychemicalromance.com, though. Part of their very expensively designed site would now feature a video game, with the character of 'Helena' from their video for the song. Deliberately 'retro' in its appeal, the game was a nostalgic take on such early video game favourites such as *Joust* and *Dig Dug*. In another retro paean, the song 'Helena' played while the gamer navigated the levels, but it was a cleverly cheesy, tinny version of the song, in line with the level of sophistication of arcade games from two decades before. In a sinister, and one might add pretty morbid twist, game players had to fight through a selection of villains, playing as the corpse and aiming to climb back in her casket. Along the way, 'Helena' had to free guarded pallbearers in an attempt to reach the next level.

'Helena' was now becoming something of a band mascot, in the same vein as Megadeth's Vic Rattlehead, Iron Maiden's Eddie and the snarling-bulldog-meets-gorilla grimace of Motörhead's very own Snaggletooth. Indeed, MCR were to top themselves (no pun intended) by re-creating the character for their fans in the United Kingdom to see in the flesh – sort of. The band were scheduled to play two shows in one day at the London Astoria and while fans waited outside the venue they were amazed to see a hearse pull down the street. Following the vehicle was a procession of fans doused in black and wearing Victorian clothing. Inside the hearse was a real coffin, in which – surrounded by bouquets of flowers – lay the young lady who had played the cadaver in the original 'Helena' video. These flowers would also shape part of the band's stage set for the concert.

With the success of this rather clever promotional stunt, MCR knew they could take the character even further and so let slip plans to create a more theatrical stage show in the future, with film props and dancers. Clearly, MCR's take on gothic imagery was just warming up.

ChAPTeR 9

Burst Spleen Titans

"What draws us is the fact that we get to see the entire world. We had always hoped to see just the country and then we got the opportunity to see the whole world, and we have really. I mean, there's lots of places we haven't been but we've been to so many places that were really high on my list and were more important to me like Japan and London, that's like a dream come true. So I think that's what drew us, the fact that we weren't gonna just be these guys that lived in our parents basements any more, we're gonna be guys who saw the world and experienced things and grew up a lot as people." Gerard Way

With their burgeoning reputation, it was inevitable, that My Chemical Romance would soon hit their home country on a huge tour, the kind attempted only by the biggest punk-rock breakthrough acts. And so it proved when they were

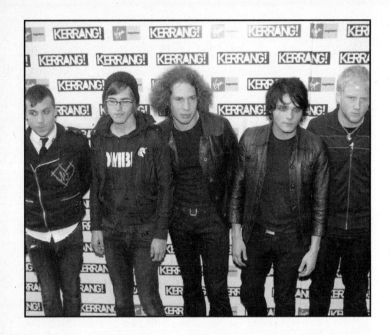

invited to join the 48 date Vans Warped tour. The shows
kicked off on June 17, 2005, at the Germain
Amphitheatre in Columbus, Ohio. MCR were the co-
headliners along with pop punksters Offspring, on a bill
that also encompassed The Transplants, Dropkick
Murphys, Thrice, Senses Fail and others. "We're not a
festival band, playing during the day was something we
had to get over, I was like, 'Uhh this sun stuff kind of
sucks,'" Gerard would later joke. He had recently
chopped his chin-length jet-black hair into a short do for
the 'Ghost Of You' video and had also significantly
slimmed down. (At one point, his weight had ballooned
to almost 200 pounds – not ideal for his five-foot eight-
inch frame.)

The tour was largely successful, yet there were inevitably negative incidents as well, all of which Gerard took in typically good spirits. At one show on the tour *Rolling Stone* reported several "college age dudes" approaching the front man, who became tense. "You suck!" one shouted, followed by "Emo sucks!" Then came one last "You suck!", for good measure. Gerard later observed wryly, "I was once that exact kid, the one who came into the city from Jersey to hang out on St Marks Place and act like a punk." Generally the singer was far more likely to be noticed by genuine fans of the band, and though this kind of attention was obviously far more welcome, it was still something of a culture shock for the shy vocalist. Typical of the brazen performer who went crazy onstage but retained an air of quiet politeness off it, Gerard was in many ways never really cut out for personal attention – though as the singer in a band who had sold almost a million copies of its second album, and with his distinctive death-warmed-up pallor, he was difficult *not* to recognise.

Sometimes, things became a little too intense and personal, though. Gerard told www.straight.com about one MCR show in Chicago on the Warped Tour: "I accidentally smashed my face wide open. My teeth were rammed through my lip, there was blood everywhere, and I was holding a rag filled with ice to my face. I come off-stage and someone asks me to take a picture. I was like, 'Are you out of your fucking mind?'"

In fact, perhaps in part due to Gerard's new lifestyle – but more likely just because the band were big kids – My Chemical Romance had become one of the least 'rock 'n' roll' bands on the road come 2005. At the beginning of the Warped tour, the band made one of their regular trips to a Columbus Wal-Mart to stock up on diet soda, cereal, horror movies and, without a hint of irony, Spider-Man pyjama bottoms. "There have been tours where we hit a different Wal-Mart almost every night," Gerard told *Rolling Stone*, as he and Mikey headed straight to the toy department. The Way brothers were reported to "carefully scrutinise" several *Star Wars* action figures. Yet Gerard had something far more important on his mind as he trekked with his cart to the office supplies section, as he explained to the magazine: "I need one of those plastic magazine racks," he said, "so I can organise my *Dungeons and Dragons* books." Therein lay the beauty of My Chemical Romance: they were still just big kids and the suggestion that fame had gone to their head was never going to come from anyone who knew how they really were in everyday life. No cocaine-smothered groupies for this band, they wanted snacks and magazine racks.

> *"I need one of those plastic magazine racks," he said, "so I can organise my Dungeons and Dragons books."*

In fact, not content with nightwear in the style of Peter Parker's alter ego, this band actually had *Teen Titans* bed sheets on their tour bus bunks. The show, another Cartoon Network creation, was all about five teenage superheroes who according to the official website, "Fight aliens, evil doers and dirty dishes all for the good of humanity." Considering that the lyrics of Gerard Way often focused on 'bad guys', it was no surprise that in real life Way harboured a childlike and refreshing innocence – in many respects, it was as if he was simply refusing to grow old.

"I don't think that having a My Chemical Romance action figure will make a kid start his own band."

Whether ironically or deadpan serious (one suspects the latter), the members of My Chemical Romance like to think of themselves as comic-book characters – superheroes, no less. Hence, it was no surprise that while MCR were on the Warped jaunt, SEG Tours suggested the band should have action figures of themselves produced for posterity. How could they refuse such an offer? "I don't think that having a My Chemical Romance action figure will make a kid start his own band. I like to think it will make him save children from a burning building," said Gerard, referring to his group's superhero status. The action figures (the band hated the term 'dolls') would eventually appear in late 2005. SEG had previously designed the extremely popular Metallica and Good Charlotte dolls, as well as models of MCR's ol' buddies Green Day. The figures were five inches tall, sold separately and each carried a red hand gun and a coffin. Gerard even designed a special and very exclusive 'prayer card' to be sold with the dolls at popular goth/punk store Hot Topic. Anyone who managed to score an extremely limited-edition 'zombie' version of the figures should count themselves lucky, as one was inserted randomly into one of every eight packages. And there was no chance MCR was about to be blitzed by commercialism and hire others to do their work for them. According to Gerard Way, interviewed for *Concert Live Wire*, MCR, "have a say in absolutely every asset of the band and that's probably why we get worn out. We approve, some of them we flat out design. Some we get our friends to design. So yeah, we're involved in everything from what goes on the kick-drum head." Punk rock had never tasted so good.

* * * * *

Meantime, Frank Iero was not resting on his laurels as a member of My Chemical Romance. The guitarist started an organisation he called Skeleton Crew, which was a record label, book publishing company and clothing design label. "If we're going to do it, we might as well do it all," Iero argued. "Skeleton Crew Records will put out limited-edition releases, coloured vinyl, picture discs, and things I would want as a record collector. Basically whatever the band wants to do, we will put out. Some of the bands you might have heard of, some of the bands you might not have. The one thing they will all have in common is that we like them, which means they are worth checking out.

"Skeleton Crew Publications will release books written or illustrated by musicians," he continued, "artists, athletes, and just all around interesting people who have something to say. We are creating a different forum where art and ideas can be presented. With media some of these artists have not experimented with or explored yet. We will not censor any of the artists, they will have full rein over what they create." Iero was adamant that his Skeleton Crew clothing line was not a T-shirt company, though. He stressed he had nothing against companies producing T-shirts, but at the back of his mind it was clear he did not want to be labelled as the head of some tacky organisation, and due to that, SC clothing pledged to develop a full range of products for all seasons. Says Iero, "You will be able to wear nothing but Skeleton Crew products for weeks, straight to any occasion or destination and never think twice about whether your uniform is comfortable, appropriate, or fashionable. The designs are rad." And what's more, he added, "This is a business that has a greater good in mind, Skeleton Crew will donate a portion of all profits to different charitable organisations, decided upon by the artists we work with."

Charity was clearly not on the mind of MCR's old ally, The Used's Bert McCracken, when he made a cryptic comment to MTV: "I'd prefer to say nothing more about My Chemical Romance, except that we did have a falling out. We don't speak at all any more.

It's got nothing to do with their success. I'm completely comfortable with where our band is at. We used to be very close, but no more... The rest of my band, they're still mates with all the guys in that band. But I'd prefer to say nothing more about My Chemical Romance."

Gerard's take on the bust-up was that he no longer wanted to hang around with anyone who was using drugs and alcohol at a certain level, and had ended his friendship with McCracken so as not to become tempted by any more excess. With awful sadness, McCracken's ex-girlfriend Kate had died in 2004, while carrying his child. Completely aside from any apparent falling out with MCR, the horror of this personal tradegy is so vast that unless a person has experienced it, one can only imagine the devastating impact it would have on someone's life.

"The rest of my band, they're still mates with all the guys in that band. But I'd prefer to say nothing more about My Chemical Romance."

Back to the supposed fall out, it was a great shame that two breath-takingly good bands who had been great friends were rumoured to no longer be talking. It seemed so out of keeping with both acts that there should be any tension. A few months later, however, the rest of MCR stated the situation was not as serious as it seemed and that they were indeed still talking to Bert. Well, they may have been talking, but were they hanging out together any more?

"I remember one time in the studio, saying to Gerard, 'Dude, seriously, you know how much bigger you're going to be than Thursday?' ... Now, I call him, and I'm like, 'Remember when I told you that?' I just had no idea it was going to be this big.'"

At least MCR and Gerard in particular could console themselves with the happier ties they still enjoyed with Thursday and Geoff Rickly. "I sort of helped My Chem start their whole thing up and now that they're huge, I don't want to exploit that," Rickly said to MTV. "He's a friend of mine, and if it ended up seeming exploitative, like he did something with us and the label wanted to use it as a single, it would be too weird." As for My Chemical Romance's success, Rickly claimed he knew all along the band would make a major impact. "I remember one time in the studio, saying to Gerard, 'Dude, seriously, you know how much bigger you're going to be than Thursday?' and he started blushing and being like, 'Stop it, dude, I have confidence. You don't need to tell me ridiculous stuff like that,'" Rickly laughed. "Now, I call him, and I'm like, 'Remember when I told you that?' I just had no idea it was going to be *this* big."

ChAPteR 10

A Feat Of Fury

"Someone gave me a piece of really good advice when we first started. He said, 'Stop writing songs for a new record, you write songs that you want to play live. You're a band that, first and foremost, write songs to play live, so just start writing songs for yourself.' We've always felt that way so we're never thinking of the next record and that's why we're ahead of the game. By the time we got to pre-production on Three Cheers For Sweet Revenge *we were all set to go."* Gerard Way

With only two albums to their name, My Chemical Romance had established themselves as leading lights of all manner of new heavy rock scenes. Along the way the group had battled enough demons to sink lesser outfits, yet they had held firm and it seemed there was going to be nothing to stop them progressing further and becoming an all-time classic act. To do that, they would need to negotiate the so-called 'difficult third album' phase – well known in the music industry as a telling marker of whether a band will go from strength to strength or fold. Making a great third album was crucial to a band's reputation, particularly when that outfit had become notorious almost as their debut record hit the shelves.

"We've written five to six skeletons of songs. We're trying to get to a level where we can get the songs into the studio and sort of flesh them out in there."

That said, MCR didn't seem to be feeling any particular pressure about putting together that all-important third album. True, they'd been composing material on the road: "We've written five to six skeletons of songs. We're trying to get to a level where we can get the songs into the studio and sort of flesh them out in there," Ray Toro told MTV. "We're always writing because we're dying to finish a new record." Gerard Way was positively bullish about the future: "I feel so extremely confident in the direction we're moving in, because we made a great leap from *I Brought You My Bullets You Brought Me Your Love,* to *Three Cheers For Sweet Revenge,* and that leap can be even greater now."

The leap from the debut to the follow-up had been, according to the band at least, a cross between a natural progression and a huge jump, and they felt they were making the same kind of leap again towards the material set to be on the third album. It was an ambitious assertion and the pressure was therefore all the greater for the band to deliver. It was not simply fans who knew or cared about the band's movements – now there was the small matter of the world's music press. The latter had bestowed some kind of new messiah status on My Chemical Romance, convinced that here was a group who could bridge the mainstream while maintaining their credibility. For anyone who heard the way MCR talked about themselves, or their fans, it was difficult to argue.

"There's just so much I want to say about real life now," Way said to www.pluggedinonline.com of his new lyrics. "We're starting to see the beauty of the world and to truly understand our relationships with other human beings, like our loved ones. What's wrong with writing a song about missing somebody instead of vampire assassins? There's a common saying in My Chemical Romance that 'This is bigger than us', but what I've come to realise is that, at the same time, there's nothing bigger than the lives of the five guys in this band." All five band members knew the sky was the limit with regards to the material they could create, and to exactly how far they could take their music, their image and their reputation. MCR were now more than merely a rock band; they were rapidly becoming an institution. "We might even have a ballad on the next record,"

Gerard told *Designer*, sounding warning bells for some of his more narrow-minded fans, perhaps, but absolutely adamant about his band's ability – and right – to go where it pleased. "Within this band you can do anything you want because when it comes down to the five of us playing, it will sound like My Chemical Romance. I think this time round I will be a little more direct [about] notions like salvation, retribution, damnation and how the band saved my life. I definitely want to deal with those subjects as opposed to something fictitious."

The band, Gerard in particular, were often asked how they viewed their own success. With typical good grace, the response would be humble, respectful and honest. As Gerard told one reporter, "I think it's pretty incredible and it's really a testament to not only the human spirit, but just the fact that people were again for real music… we saw a lot of our friends unfortunately get the shit knocked out of them by commercial radio and record labels. We saw a lot of our friends go through the ringer and it was upsetting to us. And we saw a lot of bands ripping off our friends and getting huge and it kind of bummed us out. In a way we kinda felt that it was our mission to make it work in any way possible. We think that it's a beautiful thing that people want to see this band succeed because they feel it's a valid band." Yet despite his inherent good nature, he offered a terse riposte to the band's detractors during an interview with *Alternative Press*: "If people know anything about this band they would know that we ate shit, got sick, slept on wood floors, caught flues – we did the whole thing for, like, two and half years with no promise of ever getting big and no desire to ever be giant. It was just like, 'Let's just be this band.' I think anybody that becomes more educated about this band understands a little more where we're coming from when we say things like that."

"I think it's pretty incredible and it's really a testament to not only the human spirit, but just the fact that people were again for real music..."

My Chemical Romance would always be Gerard's priority of course, but almost inevitably he sometimes considered returning to his other main passion, comic books. He had already designed the entire booklet and inner tray pictures for *Three Cheers For Sweet Revenge*. The cover, titled 'Demolition Lovers II', was a blood-spattered but still touching study of two lovers. The tray card – titled 'Just The Way It Goes' by Gerard – was a portrayal of the 'Helena' character on an operating table, with blood-spotted sheets and surgical tools, as if she had just passed away, or was going through a post mortem. In keeping with the dark nature of the band, this picture was sinister, yet still pretty. It was clear that Gerard was a talented illustrator and he had certainly been through a lifetime of training in order to become a full-time artist. The question was, which did he want more – art or music? The singer revealed to *NME* that he had written a comic entitled *The Umbrella Brigade*: "Obviously, [with] my being in My Chemical Romance, there's going to be a certain number of issues that people are going to buy but I don't want to have it as another merch item for people to buy and I'm not going to sell it at shows probably. I don't want it connected to the band," he added, "because then I feel that that would just be corny and just exploiting something that's happening with the band right now. I'm very excited, I'm going to do all the design work for it and write, and unfortunately I can't draw it because of schedule.

"Ever since I got clean and sober I have nine extra hours every day that I have nothing to really do with."

"Ever since I got clean and sober I have nine extra hours every day that I have nothing to really do with," he went on. "I have a lot of press to do, that's one thing that happens often, and then some days it's like a driving day off and then we get somewhere and I have eight hours. I can either go to the mall or I can go write comics. I find that ever since I got sober that I just have this desire to create again and be involved in comics so I'm very excited about it."

Luckily for Gerard, the rest of the band were all comic fans, and he always had one or more on hand to give their knowledgeable and respected opinion. Gerard would claim he often bounced ideas off Frank and particularly his brother Mikey. "I'd definitely like to get Mikey involved to assist me with some of the story lines," he told *Crush Music*, "because he has a really bizarre way of thinking and it's very much unlike anybody else I've ever met, so I'm sure he'll come up with some. I want to do a very bizarre comic."

For those not in the know, the *Watchmen* series referred to was the now legendary twelve-issue comic written by Alan Moore. The comics were initially released separately in 1986 and 1987 but would later be reissued as one graphic novel, which would be heralded as a masterpiece and a benchmark in the history of adult-oriented comics. Comic expert and writer Don Markstein wrote, "What *The Maltese Falcon* did for detective stories and *Shane* did for Westerns, *Watchmen* did for superheroes. It transcended its origins in what was previously considered a lowbrow form of fiction to provide a rich reading experience for all, whether they came in as fans of the genre or not." Gerard Way most probably admired it, but doubtless he would not want his own work to be considered derivative of such a well-known and much-respected publication. It seems highly likely that if Gerard does indeed manage to publish his comic book ideas, they will prove to be hugely popular – not only does he have a huge fanbase eager to see what he creates next, but the genre has never been more popular, helped by massive blockbuster remakes of old comic book favourites such as The Incredible Hulk, various Batman movies, Spider-man, The Fantastic Four and many others.

Will Gerard realise his comic-book dreams? Watch this space. But you wouldn't want to bet against it... would you?

CHAPTER 11

Transcending The Expected

"Getting big was never really a goal. It's just kind of one of those nice things that happened. For whatever reason, people connected with our music. So where things are now, you know, if everything went away tomorrow, you know, we would all be happy and proud. If things go further then things go further. That's how things are." Ray Toro

In a period of just four years, My Chemical Romance had fully established themselves on the heavy rock scene and had exceeded even their own wildest expectations. Perhaps deep in the recesses of his mind, Gerard Way had been convinced that the band could transcend their original humble goals, but for the other members every day was a blessing and they weren't about to let it go, or forget what it had taken to get them this far. "When we started this band we set mini goals and then we had our ultimate goal," Frank Iero admitted to www.lifeinabungalow.com. "We met all our smaller goals: we've gotten to meet and work with some of our heroes, and we've been able to reach an exorbitant amount of kids that we never thought we would ever reach. Our major goal was to actually make a difference, and I think we are on our way to that goal." For his part, manager Brian Schechter admitted, "It's been a pretty wild ride, especially being a first-time manager with the band and them being a first-time major label band. To remember moments and look back at everything we've done together and what the band has done to get to the point that they are, it's just an incredible feeling."

> ## *"When we started this band we set mini goals and then we had our ultimate goal."*

But it was Gerard who had changed most – and in all respects for the better. Remarkably, he did not consider himself a particularly talented musician, believing himself to be a self-made artist rather than a natural one, an idea perhaps influenced by the fact that his grandmother nurtured his artistic tendencies. With such built-in insecurity, coupled with the creative tendencies that place him equally at home singing or making art,

Gerard will always be a fascinating artist. Yet he feels safer having My Chemical Romance to guide him through the darker times: "If I hadn't found this band I would probably still be very unhappy," he said to *Designer*. "I would probably still be drinking. I would probably be in a slump. I'm 27 now so I would be 27 and felt like I have done nothing. You start to hit that point around 25 and that's right when things started to turn round for me. I'd been feeling lost since I was about 22 because I would always put a lot of pressure on myself, I'd been depressed and the band in many ways was a last-ditch effort." There are many who have felt this way about music, and their own bands in particular, and some never make it. Perhaps they end up on the streets, in jail, on welfare or worst of all, working a dead-end job with no hope and little enjoyment out of life. For all the downsides of life in a touring rock band, Gerard knew it sure beat the alternatives.

And his more mellow lifestyle is certainly more preferable to a life scurrying from city to city in a tour bus, frequently partying to excess. For the MCR vocalist, life is about learning and he is a great believer in improving one's personality through both failures and victories. He'd originally failed to make much of an impact as a comic artist, and a cartoon creator, but subliminally the singer must have learned some valuable lessons from the experience. It simply made him a stronger, better performer – quite clearly, without him My Chemical Romance would not be such a colossus. That said, the other members make an invaluable contribution to the overall MCR experience, and together they are a unit which is capable of moving into whichever musical realm they please. They are not afraid to experiment and remain fearless of how they are perceived, because of their solidarity as a group. Their experiences have seen them travel through adversity that's far greater than a few people thinking they suck, or someone disliking their image.

Ray Toro summed up the band's thankfulness for their career so far when he observed, "I can definitely say that where we are now, I'd be happy if it stayed like this forever." The chances of the band retaining their credibility and success are high. My Chemical Romance really does exist for a greater reason other than merely playing music for their own needs, or as a money-grabbing machine. For them, the band has become a symbol, a Samaritan cause set to raucous music that gets people pumped up, makes them laugh, cry and every emotional variant in-between. "We are extremely sincere about our music," Gerard told *The Punk Site*, "and you can kind of hear that as a result in the music... we're also a band who takes a lot of risks musically, and I think that's the most exciting part of listening to this band. From our standpoint, we listen to it like fans, you know? We're all fans of the band we're in and the fact that each song is completely different from the last, you never know what we're gonna do next, I think is really exciting about us."

In some ways however, Gerard and MCR knew exactly what they were going to do next. Just as when he was touting the idea of a band to his friend, Gerard had now figured out a schedule for the band by which they would live their next few years. He suggested they would "put out a new record after the next one. We'll probably put out another record after this then tour extensively on it. Then I'd like to see the band take a break for a little while to re-evaluate themselves as individuals and as a band and to kind of evolve again as a band. I think that really needs to happen and I think some of that stuff only happens from breaks. I see us probably as almost a completely different sounding band with the same ethics. Maybe on a different level I'm not really sure. I know we'll still be doing this, though."

One certainty was that a soon-to-be-released documentary film would provide the deepest insight into My Chemical Romance yet. The piece was a year in the making and covered the rise of the group from little-known brash punks to regular guests on TRL (the hit and hip MTV live request show). "It's a documentary that captures the rise and occasional stumblings of this band," explained Gerard to MTV. "It's really crazy, we had forgotten about a lot of the stuff that happens in the film, like backstage stuff and concert footage. Basically, it tells the story of one really crazy year in this band's life." The documentary, to be titled *Life On The Murder Scene* hit stores in March 2006, and coincided with the band beginning serious work on their follow-up to *Three Cheers For Sweet Revenge*. The documentary would be but a small part of the ...*Murder Scene* release. Altogether there were to be two DVDs and a live CD with the tracks taken from the group's *MTV2 $2 Bill* performance. There would also be a session that the band taped for AOL, a gig from New Jersey's Starland Ballroom plus studio demos and one unreleased track, 'Desert Song', which was the sole leftover from the *Three Cheers for Sweet Revenge* sessions.

Aside from the main DVD documentary disc there was an accompanying disc bursting with MCR goodies – live footage from the *$2 Bill* show and the Starland gig, TV appearances (*Late Night With Conan O'Brien* and MTV's *Discover and Download*), performances taped for various online music outlets, plus the music videos for "I'm Not Okay (I Promise)' and 'Helena', with additional behind-the-scenes footage filmed on the sets of those videos. It was a lavish presentation of a group still in its early stages, but no more than My Chemical Romance deserved.

After all, they are now a massive band in their own right and the world is their oyster. The only question left to answer now, is: just how big will they become?

ChAPteR 12

Bottling It

Just how big will they become…? Before My Chemical Romance could answer that question, there seemed to be more concerns about whether the band would still exist by the end of 2006 than whether they would continue their ascendancy. The reason for these doubts? The aforementioned and brilliantly insightful DVD release, *Life On The Murder Scene*. Hitting the shelves just after the first edition of this book, the long-awaited behind-the-scenes chronicle of the band was all that it had promised to be … and then some.

The DVD contained all the usual elements, lots of live footage, both audio and visual, TV and on-line appearances as well as demo tracks, an unreleased song and all the videos from *Three Cheers For Sweet Revenge* – including the 'making of…' all three clips. There was plenty of information even the most ardent fan may not have known – and above all there were warm compliments from each member for their band mates. The DVD begins with character profiles of each MCR representative. However, undoubtedly the most fascinating part for fans was the two-hour 'Video Diary'. This was essentially a magnifying glass scrutinising all things My Chemical Romance. It was a chance for fans to finally see behind the scenes of the band as well as having a permanent record of their heroes.

Yet even the most diehard MCR fan was shocked by the revelations contained on the disc. It was common knowledge that Gerard had been drinking heavily, especially on the road, but the extent to which this had come to interfere with life in MCR was only fully revealed here, for the first time. The band's manager gave compelling interviews about Gerard's issues with drink and there was even shocking footage of the singer stumbling around very much the worse for wear, eventually falling to the ground in a sniggering heap. The DVD made it quite clear that Gerard had successfully taken control of this situation and was comprehensively back on form, but nonetheless it was a quite dramatic and unnerving spectacle, not least because the band had had the bravery to include this footage on their own release. For the band's fanbase, here was a man to whom they looked for reassurance and guidance and so it was incredibly bold of the group to show their own cracks and flaws.

On a positive note, the DVD revealed more about what Gerard's home looks like, his bedroom, his time drawing graphic novels and what it was like to be in the MCR tour bus. Unlike many musical subjects on DVD, the band seemed completely unphased by the presence of cameras and were thus portrayed as both approachable and affable. It was also interesting to see the band name-check their influences so enthusiastically, in true homage to old heroes: Black Flag, The Misfits and The Smiths all received strong praise, along with Gerard's personal childhood favourites, Iron Maiden. Revealingly The Smiths were described by Gerard as "bleak pop". He also hinted that this is the bar MCR had been aiming for themselves – and it's certainly not a stretch to suggest MCR play their own brand of bleak pop music. But of course the New Jersey band features several aspects that make them very different to Morrissey and cohorts. The most obvious is the opposing styles of the two guitar players [whereas The Smiths relied solely on the genius of Johnny Marr for six-string music], a contradiction which Frank Iero even references in the video diary, suggesting he and Ray Toro have different styles that "shouldn't work, but do."

One of the points that the band was keen to make and, to anyone who had seen them live at the smaller venues they used to frequent, they made no differential between playing a 300-capacity gig or a 3000 seater. They were sticklers for providing value for money.

However, this earnest and admirable dedication

would soon be questioned in the most testing and dangerous of ways.

While their fanbase were busy watching *Life On The Murder Scene*, the band were holed up in the studio recording their next album. Two years on the road was seen as no excuse not to throw themselves straight into the next project. Given the success of the preceding record, most observers were expecting the third record to be more of the same.

How wrong could they be?

Back in 2002, My Chemical Romance's debut album had featured a future classic in the song 'Headfirst For Halos'. With its upbeat energy, this track felt almost out of place on a record full of cathartic outpourings. Yet, as Gerard Way would say during *Life On The Murder Scene*, that very song stopped the band being pigeonholed. The group worked hard to complete that track, and there were even doubters within the MCR camp at the time that worried the song would not be in their best interests.

It was, in fact, vital for their future. Why?

Firstly, because that one song set the band apart from the emo crowd. Secondly it gave MCR full licence to try almost anything on their future material without anyone being surprised or myopically critical. 'Headfirst For Halos' was a key stepping stone that would, just four years later, pave the way for My Chemical Romance to make their most ambitious album to date.

When sessions started for the new record in April 2006, the band as much as anyone, was acutely aware that their commercial success with the second album had in turn placed unavoidable preconceptions from the public and media alike about what an MCR song 'sounded like'. The band had solidified their camaraderie with a couple of years of touring, they had seen there were connections between certain songs/choruses/lyrics at every concert, they knew there were certain song parts guaranteed to make people go crazy. It would have been all too easy for MCR to use this knowledge to create their most bouncy, catchy and anthemic recording to date. But in typical fashion, My Chemical Romance thought 'Fuck it – let's just make the *best* album we can.' The working title for the new album was originally thought to be *The Rise and Fall of My Chemical Romance*, but in an interview with *Kerrang!*, Gerard dismissed this monicker as no more than "a spoof, or joke."

Perhaps surprisingly, the band did not work with Howard Benson again, instead choosing Rob Cavallo who most recently had presided over the multi-platinum, globally massive punk concept album, *American Idiot*, which elevated that particular trio to god-like, stadium-filling status around the world. The producer had also worked with Less Than Jake and Avril Lavigne so he brought a breadth of pop and punk influences to the studio. Sessions were fast, productive and intense. MCR could feel they were creating something very special.

The upside of MCR's commercial success was the control they could now display over their music. There was no need to lay down music that would take over the world/smash the charts/please a record label. Yet there were pitfalls to be avoided that certain other bands had encountered. The Rasmus, for instance, blew up to gargantuan proportions with their breakthrough record *Dead Letters* but could not maintain the momentum and by the time of their follow-up album many of their fans had moved on. But would that happen with My Chemical Romance?

> *"One of the most annoying characteristics of teenagers is their refusal to open their curtains. Their world is dark and airless."*

The chasm between middle-class banality and rock and roll's incendiary edges has long been a source of conflict and controversy. From Elvis's hip-swivelling, through The Beatles' 'outrageous' haircuts, on through the Sex Pistols establishment baiting and on and on... every generation and pretty much every major musical movement has had it critics. Music like this, so say the chattering classes, corrupts the feeble minds of our youth, infects society with amoral ethics and generally is just not cricket. This was a common stance from such organisations as the PMRC (Parents Music Resource Center) which, in the late 1980s and early 1990s sought to relegate the heavy metal music scene to a cavern underground by first criticising all manner of bands and musicians involved with the genre, and later successfully campaigning for all albums with 'explicit lyrics' to have a sticker on the front cover to warn parents about the dangers within.

A bastion of similar conservatism is *The Daily Mail*. Caught between the broadsheets and the red top tabloids, the newspaper was well-known for running articles on 'yoof cultcha'. On August 17, 2006, the writer Sarah Sands ran an 'expose' of the emo movement, name checking MCR in a rather ridiculous article that criticised the movement generally for its effect on children who, apparently, were driven to suicidal thoughts at emo's evil hands.

Among the deeply insightful (!) theories put forward were such revelations as, "one of the most annoying characteristics of teenagers is their refusal to open their curtains. Their world is dark and airless. If this environment is coupled with the psychological traits of self-pity, introspection, self-dramatisation and hormone imbalance, you have a fully-fledged Emo, even without the small T-shirt and black hair…" Seemingly oblivious to this teenage aptitude having existed for decades rather than since the second My Chemical Romance album, Sands went on to suggest that, "What worries me is that teenagers are less equipped to manage strong emotions and a cult of suicide could have real and horrible consequences. It is irresponsible for the fashion and music cultures to encourage it."

In fact, what was deeply disturbing was that an article could misinterpret and misrepresent a 'movement' (if indeed there was one) and certain bands so badly.

Anyone who had been to a MCR gig would know that Gerard was at pains to bolster the fans who might be suffering from low self-esteem, to encourage those who were struggling with issues and, above all, make a generation of outsiders feel like they belonged somewhere … anywhere.

Perhaps most disturbingly, all that Sands's article probably achieved was to convince paranoid (and misinformed) parents that emo music was dangerous and should be taken away from their children to keep them safe. And in doing so, they would therefore be removing what might be in some cases the only sanctuary an emotionally uncertain teenager has.

The thrust of the article led to fierce debate on the internet, in chatrooms, on Myspace, *everywhere*, about the merits or otherwise of 'emo' and when *NME* chipped in with the front cover 'War On Emo!', the controversy had become a fully-fledged battle. My Chemical Romance – along with Panic! At The Disco, Taking Back Sunday and (oddly) Fall Out Boy – were right in the firing line.

"That was a very negative article written about the band and the band's fans and it was completely ignorant," Gerard later said. "It was unfounded, there was no factual information at all. We do not promote self-harm but we encourage kids to find other ways to get out their frustrations. We represent the exact opposite."

Thankfully not every reader of that newspaper condoned the article and sense prevailed from one particular mother who felt aggrieved enough to send in a letter defending her daughter's right to listen to so-called emo music and specifically one band in particular. "I have a teenage daughter who possibly would not be here today if it weren't for the love and support of one of the bands mentioned in this article – My Chemical Romance," she wrote. "Bands like this provide a forum for teenagers to talk about their feelings, and also give a sense of belonging which is so often missing in everyday life for them." It gives some encouragement to all young rock fans, who find themselves isolated, that when a parent can recognise wayward and ill-informed journalism, there is hope for everyone.

"The funny thing is that I've met more kids that have stopped self-harming because of us, than anything."

"The funny thing is that I've met more kids that have stopped self-harming because of us, than anything. That's the case with most of the kids I meet, especially in the UK, so I guess it is some sort of epidemic. Most of the kids that I meet, that say thank you, are kids that used to self-harm. Papers like that (*The Daily Mail*) will never do their homework, but it is kind of funny to call it 'emo death cult', or whatever it was called."

It was clear that emo divided lovers of music. For example, when *NME* took the bold step of placing Illinois lightweights Fall Out Boy on their front cover, the letters mailbag was inundated. For a magazine more used to placating fans with slightly less mainstream pop acts, the reaction to Fall Out Boy's inclusion was gargantuan. In fact the letters were some of the most severe *NME* had ever received in 54 years of music coverage. By declaring particular bands to be part of this specific type of alternative music, this allowed narrow-minded fans, 'indie fascists' if you will, to pigeon-hole the enemy. Most bands were actually far more intelligent than a simple genre classification could suggest. For their part, at first My Chemical Romance felt aggrieved at this article but distant from it too, because they saw themselves no more an emo band than a disco group.

MCR didn't feel they had anything to fear from emo bashers.

Except it wasn't that simple.

Reading Festival, Bank Holiday weekend, the end of August 2006.

Picture the (murder) scene.

It was a very energised and excited MCR that played the famous, prestigious Reading Festival. Yet various websites and chatrooms prior to the event had hinted at a potential conflict with certain elements of the beer-guzzling, sun-soaking Bank Holiday crowd. There were even explicit early warnings that certain people were intent on "bottling" MCR, and that the bottles would contain various nasty substances, not least urine.

Was this going to be the most public manifestation of a war on emo? The signs for Gerard and Co were not good. When notorious emo band Panic! At The Disco were targeted, it seemed this vendetta was bigger than just My Chemical Romance. An unidentified missile was thrown at PATD's front man Brendon Urie during the first song of the band's set. The object knocked him unconscious though thankfully it was only a short time before he regained composure and bravely finished the set. Urie took the incident in good spirits, telling *NME*: "I'm doing alright now. I could be way worse, I could be dead. What I remember is I got hit, got knocked out, woke up and finished the set. We just got on with it. I guess we were sending a message to whoever threw the bottle: you can't stop us!"

That was exactly the type of reaction the detractors did not want, considering they were trying their level best to disrupt the band's rhythm and get them to walk offstage or worse, assault the audience member responsible. Nonetheless, as admirable as PATD's reaction was, the assault on Urie reminded everyone who had been keeping an eye on the alternative music forums that there could be more violence and it might well be directed at My Chemical Romance.

It was.

MCR had transcended their humble origins and as such the target on their collective backs was increasing in size by the day. It would perhaps make a 'statement' if they were the band that certain elements of the crowd managed to humiliate. When heavy metal behemoths

Slayer had finished a triumphant set, (completely at odds with most bands on the Festival bill), MCR followed. They were welcomed by the majority of people in attendance but there was a substantial element of rabble rousers who decided to pelt the band with everything from rotten fruit and golf balls to bottles of urine. Not only was this highly dangerous, it was doubtless going to be a prominent news story and that just served to increase the severity of the attacks, with the brainless buoyed by the collective angst directed at Gerard Way in particular. The frontman however was resolutely defiant and, like Brendon Urie, took the bottling with consummate good grace. In overcoming the abuse, this difficult gig was one of their best ever. "We might be outsiders today, but we represent every outsider out there," Way rallied. "This song is called 'thanks for all the bottles, thanks for all the piss, thanks for all the golf balls, thanks for all the apples and thanks for all the sticky shit'." He even felt energised enough to lead the crowd in a chant of "Fuck the *Daily Mail*! Fuck the *Daily Mail*!"

And yet, just a year before, Gerard and company had performed at the very same festival and received a rapturous reception. So, why were they now the targets for some individuals to vent their anger? Some observers suggested that certain sections of the band's fan base felt they were becoming too commercial and they couldn't accept the ongoing popularity that was morphing MCR into a whole other entity than simply a punk rock band.

Devoted MCR fans couldn't understand it; after the show most were posting in support of their heroes, and equally there were confessed non-fans of the band who couldn't concur with the belief that MCR deserved to be bottled or booed. The general belief amongst forum posters was simple – if you don't like a band, don't watch them. Go do something else – no band deserves to be bottled, especially when there were going to be thousands of people who had paid good money to watch them.

> *"When the first bottle landed onstage at Reading my initial instinct was, 'this is going to be fun.'"*

Rather than bemoan his luck or criticise those who felt the need to launch ten tons of crap at his band, Gerard Way threw a curveball and stated that the incident was a *good* thing. Viewing the angry reception from a positive perspective, he intimated that MCR were clearly no harmless and sterile Top 20 pop band. On the contrary, My Chemical Romance could still provoke people into negative reactions and that was something to be savoured.

"When the first bottle landed onstage at Reading my initial instinct was, 'this is going to be fun,'" Gerard later commented. "We've had so many pats on the back in the U.S. and it gets to the stage where you're doing victory laps. And then what are you fighting against? If you don't have adversity, what are you? There's only love and hate with this band, nothing in the middle." Elsewhere, he said: "I think we're bigger than emo and I think all these bands and all of our fans ... are bigger than just one subgenre that's hot for a minute." Besides Gerard could afford to be confident. He knew what the band had been creating in the studio. He knew they had a secret weapon.

They were about to release an album that would make them one of the biggest bands on the planet ...

ChAPteR 13

Welcome to
the Black Parade

"If we don't fuck this up we could be legendary."
Gerard Way

E ven after the bottling at Reading, the anticipation
for MCR's new material was frantic. There had
been gossip in the media about a mysterious web
site called 'The Black Parade'; there had been industry
whispers about the new album being completely
different to anything the band had made before; there
was talk of huge record company backing for the
forthcoming project; quiet conversations about
stadiums, movies ... yet no one as yet knew what to
expect from the music.

In the last week of October, 2006, My Chemical
Romance released 'Welcome To The Black Parade', the

first single from their forthcoming album, and overnight changed their world forever. Disarming the listener immediately with slow, mournful piano stabs, before Gerard's emotional vocal starts, accompanied by a military multi-snare roll, the band was clearly making a very blunt statement … to expect the unexpected. He sings of the Black Parade, his father, phantoms and demons, very dark and very emotive. This intriguing sequence is then repeated to a growing musical climax before tumbling drums smash the song back into what, at first, sounds like fairly standard MCR fayre, the hooks, the vocal, the stabbing guitars, the ability to somehow fire energy into the veins like perhaps no other band of the moment.

But then, quite frankly, MCR go completely nuts.

After the second chorus, a 'middle-eight' [if it can be called that this late in the song], pre-empts a bombastic breakdown, with chanting vocals that then leads into what can only be described as Brian May-on-acid guitars (Gerard openly voiced his admiration of Freddie Mercury and Queen in interviews), a degree of pomp that must have had Meat Loaf pulling his hair out with envy and then the closing choruses of multi-layered vocals, crashing guitars and … just musical mayhem. The military snares close the song suddenly, leaving the listener bemused, fascinated, excited, shocked.

What a bonkers comeback.

If that wasn't enough, the video was an epic depiction of the key character of the forthcoming album, the so-called 'Patient' whose life and woes would run central to the new album. Lying in a hospital bed on the brink of death, he sees the Reaper in the guise of a marching band that his father took him to see as a child and at the forefront of that 'parade' is MCR, clad in striking military garb. However, most striking of all is Gerard's hair – gone are the black flowing locks that had made him perhaps the definitive frontman of post-Millennial rock bands. In its place was a bleach-blond crop, short, harsh, to be honest at first, odd. Fans at Reading Festival had seen this and there had been pictures in the press too, but to see it here, actually in an MCR video was quite a shock. "When we play these songs we're acting out the characters of The Black Parade," Frank Iero explained to *NME*, "sometimes you can be more honest when you have a mask on."

This was no cheap promo clip either, suggesting the rumours of serious record company bucks being funnelled in marketing MCR were true. With typical drama, even the conception of this record was fraught with incident. Shot in August with Sam Bayer as director (who could boast Nirvana's watershed 'Smells Like Teen Spirit' and Green Day's 'American Idiot' videos among his portfolio – a treat for Frank who said Cobain's 'Aneurysm' was the first song he ever played to anyone on guitar), the filming saw both Gerard and Bob suffer injury. Gerard was reported to have torn ligaments in his ankle while Bob burnt his leg and then fell ill with an infection that needed hospital monitoring. A couple of shows were cancelled and there were even false rumours on the web of the band being seriously injured in a car crash, but even these incidents could not stop the approaching juggernaut that was the new album. After the video was aired in September, following the single's first radio play earlier that month, the world was ready for the next stage of My Chemical Romance's ever-complex life.

"It's just like there's this whole new aura surrounding us since the single came out."

On August 22, 2006, the band played a special one-off show at the 1800-capacity London Hammersmith Palais – not surprisingly the gig sold out in fifteen minutes flat. Twenty people draped in black capes – like some bizarre Tolkien-esque evil spirits – stood outside the venue and walked ethereally around the locale followed by signs hailing 'The Black Parade'. The hype was reaching fever pitch. At the show itself, it was 'announced' that MCR could not play after all and would instead be replaced by 'The Black Parade', a neat, if rather obvious pseudonym for Way and Co.

Just to crank the hype up another notch, the band appeared at a rare in-store appearance at the Virgin Megastore on Oxford Street in London, where 1000 fans (many of whom had slept outside the venue the night before) witnessed them playing a handful of songs including new material such as 'Famous Last Words' and 'House Of Wolves'.

Then, on October 15, 2006, MCR's new single smashed straight into the UK charts at Number 1, their first chart-topper and, indeed, their first Top Ten hit in that country (it was still there for a second week before the vacuous pop/pap of McFly toppled it from the perch). More importantly, perhaps, the success of this expansive single perfectly whetted the collective appetite for the band's third album (one should not forget the tasty little B-side, 'Heaven Help Us', which was something of a nod to their past rather than an indication of their present and future). In retrospect, and despite the seemingly infinite new musical boundaries, it was all vintage My Chemical Romance. The perception of the band was forever changed: "It's just like there's this whole new aura surrounding us," Frank said to *Play Music* magazine. "Since the single came out … I'm not going to say that people never took us seriously but now it's deadly serious, and that's kinda cool to be honest."

For the new album there was, of course, more than just the music to be contemplated. Along the lines of Green Day's *American Idiot*, MCR had created a concept to sit alongside the tunes. The previously mentioned fictional character known only as 'The Patient' was treated to a musical biography. Along the way, many aspects of life and death were covered, as well as the after-life – if indeed it existed.

And so to *The Black Parade*, My Chemical Romance's third album. The mask that Frank had alluded to in *NME* was clearly worn by Gerard as the character in the songs excavated his emotions on the likes of 'The Sharpest Lives', digging through the hell of alcohol excess and prescription drugs. This had been evident on the *Life On The Murder Scene* DVD where Way was captured stumbling and dropping like a dead bird during one particular clip. And still, for all the improvements in production and catchy pop carnage at work on *The Black Parade*, there was a dark cloud hanging over every song – it was as if the album were somehow haunted. No surprise when you consider the collection had been recorded at Los Angeles' renowned Paramour Estate which had such an eerie allure that it had recently been used for movie shoots such as *Scream II*. One night as Gerard fell asleep, weary from recording, he felt as if he were being strangled. "He felt this pressure on his neck, and he woke up and couldn't breathe and there was something inside my wall making crazy noises," Frank Iero described. "Doors would suddenly open and slam shut. It was pretty scary, and that's why some of the stuff on the new record is very dark." He also told *Kerrang!* "I felt we were treading a think line between greatness and insanity. We were always on the brink. Always."

The sessions took several sinister turns. "There were times we really cut ourselves open," Gerard told *Kerrang!* "We cut ourselves open and saw how ugly we were inside. We had our souls drained out … I'm serious, this record tried to kill us." Central to the conflict within the band's psyche was the fact that these outsiders, these perennial non-scenesters suddenly, it could be argued, belonged to the establishment. They'd sold 2.5 million copies of the second album; they were recognisable all over the world; they went to MTV Award ceremonies; they were feted and admired ... so much for being outsiders. This caused enormous internal conflict. It created darkness.

> *"We cut ourselves open and saw how ugly we were inside. We had our souls drained out ... I'm serious, this record tried to kill us."*

The methodology of recording challenged the band too – Rob Cavallo encouraged them to write in the studio, multi-layering guitars and recording tracks song-by-song in the proposed track listing order. The boundaries were limitless. Some tracks took hours just to perfect guitar layers, such was the precise attention to detail that Rob fuelled and the band demanded.

The huge introduction known as 'The End' had a string of notes Meat Loaf would have killed for – bombastic in its pompous stadium rock vibrations, before the band entered pop punk for the main opener, 'Dead!'. The lyrics to the track showed MCR were still able to worry the corporate conservative institutions. "And wouldn't it be great if we were dead?" Gerard questions, perhaps with *Daily Mail* readers in mind.

Though Gerard's voice had a gravel edge (as if

soaked in bourbon and cigarettes, occasionally reminding the listener of Jack White) there was an ironic opposition too much of the material. Ray and Frank's guitars were often harmonised *a la* Queen and there was a stadium rock tinge to several songs, notably the potential future single, 'This Is How I Disappear'. Equally there are many moments where the quirky individualism of the band shines through, as on the 'Mama' track which had an unexpected guest vocalist in Liza Minelli. This eerie apologetic affront was epic and reminiscent of classic marching band music, proving

"There's a fine line, between kitschy joke rock and poignant, directly theatrical music with true concepts."

MCR knew its chosen theme inside out.

The new album was certainly cloaked in darkness, the likes of 'I Don't Love You' showed the rest of the rock scene how to create a filthy, distorted power ballad. The track made its point quickly, unlike most other forms of dreary pop. It was with the likes of this slightly off-kilter track, along with say 'Sleep' (that was the closest MCR got to 'filler') where the band were not fully on form. Still, their desire and fearless need to experiment made the album a captivating and perpetually rewarding listen, no small achievement given it's length at over an hour (almost double that of its predecessor).

Doubtless the most memorable tracks on *The Black Parade* are those where the band is in full rock attack mode, but it is the insertion of peculiar sounds, melodies and ideas which make the album an enjoyable and full-on concept – only one or two tracks work well outside of the album as a whole. Proof then that MCR could turn their hands to almost anything … the wonder of where they might travel next is just one reason why their fan base has been retained and increased tenfold.

To be fair, particularly given the bottling at Reading and the media criticism of emo, such a dramatic change of direction could have easily backfired. But with genuine insightful maturity, Gerard revealed the band were well aware of the pitfalls of this unlikely musical evolution: "There's a fine line," he told *Play Music*, "between kitschy joke rock and poignant, directly theatrical music with true concepts, and you have to be very careful with that. I think the best thing is to always play with people's expectations…"

The press response was genuinely ecstatic. *NME* – not renowned for being overtly pro-MCR, was gushing: 'This album is about to turn MCR into the biggest band on the planet. For now, this is one to file alongside *American Idiot*, *Doolittle* and *Nevermind* on your 'Greatest US Rock Albums' shelf. The new kings of the world'; *Kerrang!*, long-time supporters were equally keen, saying, "Flamboyance in abundance, once this record reveals its secrets to you, you will be dazzled by its brilliance'; *Total Guitar* said simply that it was 'mind-blowing'; *Total Guitar* said "It's more than good, it's astonishing" ... and so on ...

It was all the more rewarding that the album was so thoroughly critically appreciated, given everything the band had been through in order just to finish and release the record. "It was almost like the other records and tours and hardships we've been through like drugs and alcohol were a test to see if we could get to this record," Gerard told *NME*. "That's why the record is so desperate. It's so brutally honest, and it's really opening up our insides and spilling them out." The record hit Number 2 in the charts in the UK, stopped only from the top spot by Robbie Williams' critically-panned *Rudebox* offering. *The Black Parade* hurtled towards platinum within ten days and will easily be one of the biggest selling albums of 2006 all around the world.

In doing so, MCR can now experiment with anything they wish to: Frank's started Skeleton Crew, a fluid organisation that will be publishing books (by the likes of Every Time I Die vocalist Keith Buckley), making clothing lines, recording bands (such as The Mean Reds and Hot Like (A) Robot) and so on; Gerard has been in discussions about his graphic art being published; there's even talk of a My Chemical Romance musical movie. Nothing, it seems, is out of bounds.

And Gerard's new blond hair that everyone questioned? The gamble has worked. The harshness of the cut now seems a stroke of genius that single-handedly enabled the band to shrug off any preconceptions and morph themselves from a fantastic rock-punk band into a group that may yet be seen to become historically important in rock's rich tapestry.

You see, as with so much of My Chemical Romance, he knew what he was doing all along ... didn't he?

My Chemical Romance

Discography

Singles

Headfirst For Halos –
> Original Worldwide Release (April 2004)
> 20:20 TWENTYCDS004

Headfirst For Halos
Our Lady Of Sorrows (Live)
I'm Not Okay (I Promise)
> Original Worldwide Release CD 1 (March 2005)
> Wea International W692CD1

I'm Not Okay (I Promise)
You Know What They Do To Guys Like Us In Prison
(BBC Sessions Version)
I'm Not Okay (I Promise)
> Original Worldwide Release CD 2 (March 2005)
> Wea International W692CD2

I'm Not Okay (I Promise)
Bury Me In Black
You Know What They Do To Guys
Like Us In Prison (Live)
Helena

>   Original Worldwide Release (May 2005)
>   Wea International

Helena
I'm Not Okay (I Promise) (Live From AOL Sessions)
Ghost Of You

>   Original Worldwide Release CD 1 (August 2005)
>   Wea International

Ghost Of You
Helena (Live)
Ghost Of You –

>   Original Worldwide Release CD 2 (August 2005)
>   Wea International W683CD2

Ghost Of You
Helena (Live)
Cemetery Drive (Live)

Welcome To The Black Parade
Welcome To The Black Parade/Heaven Help
Us/Welcome To The Black Parade (Live)

>   Original Worldwide Release (October 2006)
>   Wea International B000IONGJU

Albums

I Brought You My Bullets, You Brought Me Your Love

Released 2002,
Reissued April 12, 2004
20:20 9866233

Tracklisting:
Romance
Honey,
This Mirror Isn't Big Enough For The Two Of Us
Vampires (Will Never Hurt You)
Drowning Lessons
Our Lady Of Sorrows
Headfirst For Halos
Skylines And Turnstiles
Early Sunsets Over Monroeville
This Is The Best Day Ever
Cubicles
Demolition Lovers

Three Cheers For Sweet Revenge

Released September 6, 2004
Wea International I527766

Tracklisting:
Helena
Give 'Em Hell, Kid

To The End
You Know What They Do To Guys Like Us In Prison
I'm Not Okay (I Promise)
The Ghost Of You
The Jetset Life Is Gonna Kill You
Interlude
Thank You For The Venom
Hang 'Em High
It's Not A Fashion Statement It's A Deathwish
Cemetery Drive
I Never Told You What I Do For A Living

The Black Parade

Released October 23, 2004

Wea International I527766 B000I5Y8ZU

Tracklisting:
The End/Dead!
This Is How I Disappear
The Sharpest Lives
Welcome To The Black Parade
I Don't Love You/House Of Wolves
Cancer
Mama
Sleep
Teenagers
Disenchanted
Famous Last Words

Scource
Acknowledgements

The following magazines and websites were very useful in compiling this work:
Alternative Press, City Beat, Concert Live Wire, Crush Music, Designer, Florida Entertainment Scene, Kerrang!, Metal Hammer, Metal Underground, NME, Pollstar, The Punk Site, Q, Rocksound, Rolling Stone, Teen Spot, Trouble Bunch.
Specifically, a brilliant article in *Alternative Press* by Leslie Simon; various superb writing on The Punk Site, and in *Crush* and *Designer* magazines.

www.mychemicalromance.com (official site)
www.amazon.co.uk
www.en.wikipedia.org
www.fan-sites.org/mychemicalromance/
www.g33kcor3.com/mcr/
www.lifeinabungalow.com
www.mtv.com
www.myspace.com/mychemicalromance
www.pluggedinonline.com
www.punknews.org
www.radiotakeover.com
www.straight.com

Photographs

Also
Available

From Independent Music Press

Also Available From Independent Music Press

"MYSPACE OR YOURS?"
THE ALTERNATIVE GUIDE TO
THE SITE THAT CHANGED THE WORLD
by Joe Shooman

On myspace.com, everyone can hear you squirm. Artists, film-makers, musicians, lonely kids looking for love ... all twists on life can be found here in their dubious glory. Myspace.com is the most powerful social force since the formation of the internet itself. Since its launch as an online social community in July 2003 by Santa Monica-based Tom Anderson, its easy-to-use interface has allowed users to upload and share music, videos, online diaries and search for users with similar interests in a way that has revolutionised not only the internet, but an entire generation's social lives. Bloggers have found love, unwise liaisons have been discovered and careers have been launched. Through interviews with bands, music industry professionals, and a host of weird and wonderful characters, the history and impact of this unique website is told for the first time in a suitably irreverent style. This is not a book for computer geeks or tech-heads, but an immensely readable and entertaining insight into the real people and bewildering stories caught up in the story of myspace.

ISBN 0 9552822 1 7   224 Pages   Paperback   £5.99   World Rights

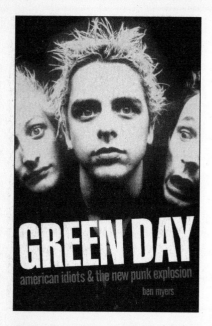

GREEN DAY: AMERICAN IDIOTS AND THE NEW PUNK EXPLOSION
by Ben Myers

The world's first and only full biography of Green Day. Self-confessed latch-key kids from small blue-collar Californian towns, Green Day have gone on to sell 50 million albums and single-handedly redefine the punk and rock genre for an entire generation. Inspired by both the energy of British punk bands as well as cult American groups, Green Day gigged relentlessly across the US underground before eventually signing to Warners and releasing their 1994 major label debut *Dookie*, which was a 10-million-selling worldwide hit album. With the arrival of Green Day, suddenly music was dumb, fun, upbeat and colourful again. Many now credit the band with saving rock from the hands of a hundred grunge-lite acts. In 2004 Green Day reached a career pinnacle with the concept album *American Idiot*, a sophisticated commentary on modern life - not least their dissatisfaction with their president. Myers is an authority on punk and hardcore and in this unauthorised book charts the band members' difficult childhoods and their rise to success, speaking to key members of the punk underground and music industry figures along the way.

ISBN 0 9539942 9 5 208 Pages Paperback, 8pp b/w pics £12.99 World Rights

DAVE GROHL: FOO FIGHTERS,
NIRVANA AND OTHER MISADVENTURES
by Martin James

The first biography of one of modern rock's most influential figures. Emerging from the morass of suicide and potent musical legacy that was Nirvana, Foo Fighters established themselves - against all odds - as one of the most popular rock bands in the world. Deflecting early critical disdain, Dave Grohl has single-handedly reinvented himself and cemented his place in the rock pantheon. This is his story, from his pre-Nirvana days in hardcore band Scream to his current festival-conquering status as a Grammy-winning, platinum-selling grunge legend reborn. Martin James once found himself watching the Prodigy backstage with Grohl, both clambering up a lighting rig to share a better view. With this in-depth book, he pieces together the life story of one of the most remarkable, enigmatic and yet amenable stars in recent music history.

ISBN 0 9539942 4 4 208 Pages Paperback, b/w pics £12.99 World Rights

Also Available From Independent Music Press

MUSE: INSIDE THE MUSCLE MUSEUM
by Ben Myers

The first and only biography of one of the most innovative and successful rock bands of recent years. Formed in the mid-1990s in a sleepy sea-side Devonshire town, Muse comprises teenage friends Matt Bellamy, Chris Wolstenholme and Dominic Howard. 2001's *Origin Of Symmetry* album spawned Top 10 hits such as 'Plug-In Baby' and a unique version of Nina Simone's classic, 'Feeling Good'. Their third album, *Absolution*, entered the UK charts at Number 1 in October 2003 – by then, all the signs were there that Muse were on the verge of becoming one of the biggest bands of the new century. Throughout 2004, they won over countless new fans at festivals, including a now-famous headline slot at Glastonbury, which preceded a two-night sell-out of the cavernous Earl's Court and a Brit Award for 'Best Live Act' in early 2005. This book tells that full story right from their inception and includes interviews conducted both with the band and those who have witnessed their climb to the top - a position they show no sign of relinquishing any time soon.

ISBN 0 9539942 6 0 208 Pages Paperback, 8pp b/w pics £12.99 World Rights

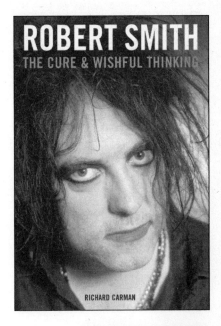

ROBERT SMITH:
THE CURE & WISHFUL THINKING
by Richard Carman

The very first in-depth biography on The Cure explores nearly thirty years of one of rock's most enduring and influential bands. Formed as The Easy Cure in 1976 by school friends Robert Smith, Lol Tolhurst and Michael Dempsey, The Cure were one of the first post-punk bands to inject pure pop back into post-Pistols rock. Throughout a career filled with paradox and evolution, endless personnel changes, and side-projects including stints with Siouxsie and the Banshees and The Glove, iconic frontman Robert Smith has kept awake and alive to changes in the music scene around The Cure. In their third decade they remain relevant and connected, when many of their contemporaries are reduced to nostalgia packages and worse. This full-length, extensively researched biography of the band, and of Smith – one of rock's most enduring figures - is the most up-to-date telling of a never-ending story; it also analyses in depth the 'goth' subculture and its relationship with The Cure.

ISBN 0 9549704 1 1 256 Pages Paperback, 8pp b/w pics £12.99 World Rights

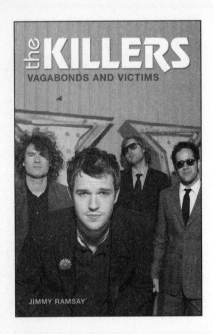

THE KILLERS: VAGABOONDS & VICTIMS
by Jimmy Ramsay

New Jersey band My Chemical Romance have taken the music underground by storm since their incendiary debut album in 2002. Within weeks of its release, major labels across the globe were frantically pulling out their cheque-books in an attempt to capture what is widely regarded as the world's next stadium-selling rock band in the vein of Metallica, Foo Fighters and Green Day. Their biting lyrics, beautiful visuals and relentless touring schedules have ensured that MCR have already captured the hearts and minds of the I-Pod generation – the year 2006 will see them promoted to the very upper echelons of rock music's giants.

This is the very first book to tell their tale, from the humble New Jersey beginnings, setting them in the context of the dormant US rock scene, through to their breakthrough live shows and meteoric success in 2004 and 2005 that sees them perched on the cusp of being a multi-million-selling global force. Mixing metal with ballads, rock with pop, MCR are the next *big* band. This book tells you how these introverted school friends achieved their dream.

ISBN 0 9549704 2 X 176 Pages Paperback, b/w pics £8.99 World Rights